Photoshop® Elements
ALL-IN-ONE DESK REFERENCE
for DUMMIES

Cheat Sheet

W9-BDV-710

File Management Shortcuts

- **Make a new file.** Ctrl+double-click the workspace.
- **Make a new image not based on the current Clipboard contents.** Press Ctrl+Alt+N.
- **Open an existing file.** Double-click the workspace.
- **Save.** Press Ctrl+S.
- **Save As.** Press Ctrl+Shift+double-click the workspace.
- **Save for Web.** Press Ctrl+Shift+Alt+S.
- **Close image.** Press Ctrl+W, or the standard Windows command Ctrl+F4.

Document Size Shortcuts

- **Image Size:** Right-click the image window title.
- **Canvas Size:** Right-click the image window title.

Layers Shortcuts

- **Duplicate a layer.** Drag the existing layer onto the New Layer icon on the Layers palette.
- **Rename a layer.** Double-click the layer title on the Layers palette and then type the name.
- **Merge layers.** Press Ctrl+E. Hidden layers are deleted.
- **Merge only visible layers.** Press Ctrl+Shift+E. Hidden layers are kept.
- **Turn a normal image into a layered image.** Double-click its thumbnail image on the Layers palette. Name it in the dialog box or accept the default name.
- **Move a layer up one in the stack.** Press Ctrl+].
- **Move a layer down one in the stack.** Press Ctrl+[.

Transformations

- **Put selection (or entire layer) into Free Transform mode.** Press Ctrl+T.
- **Apply transformations.** Press Enter.
- **Cancel transformations.** Press Esc.

Tool Shortcuts

- **Brush tool:** Press B.
- **Move tool:** Press V; also hold Ctrl.
- **Lasso tool:** Press L.
- **Marquee tool:** Press M.
- **Default swatch colors:** Press D.
- **Reverse color swatches:** Press X.
- **Hand tool:** Hold spacebar.
- **Zoom In tool:** Hold Ctrl+spacebar.
- **Zoom Out tool:** Hold Alt+spacebar.
- **Switch to precise cursor display:** Press the Caps Lock key.
- **Display palette** (most, but not all tools): Right-click in the image window.

Command Shortcuts

- **Levels:** Press Ctrl+L.
- **Hue/Saturation:** Press Ctrl+U.
- **Apply last-used filter:** Press Ctrl+F.
  Open last filter dialog box without applying filter: Press Ctrl+Alt+F.

Selections Shortcuts

- **Add to a selection** (with a selection tool chosen). Hold Shift and drag.
- **Subtract from a selection** (with a selection tool chosen). Hold Alt and drag.
- **Load a selection based on layer's opaque contents.** Ctrl+click a layer's thumbnail.
- **Invert selection.** Press Ctrl+Shift+I.
- **Select All.** Press Ctrl+A.
- **Deselect marquee.** Press Ctrl+D.

For Dummies: Bestselling Book Series for Beginners

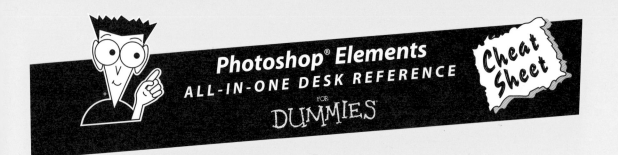

Photoshop® Elements
ALL-IN-ONE DESK REFERENCE
FOR
DUMMIES

Cheat Sheet

Standard Windows Shortcuts

- **Copy:** Press Ctrl+C.
- **Cut:** Press Ctrl+X.
- **Paste:** Press Ctrl+V.

- **Print:** Press Ctrl+P.
- **Exit Elements:** Adobe, press Ctrl+Q; Windows, press Alt+F4. Both work.

You also have at your command the contextual menu (essentially the Windows/right-click shortcut menu) for Elements. This menu changes options depending upon the active tool. My advice for independent exploration is to

- Right-click everything in the program to see what pops up.
- Double-click everything in the program to see what pops up.

- Hold Ctrl, Alt, or Shift when using a tool to see how the keys modify the tool behavior.

Changing the Window Background

Occasionally, I want to see what an image looks like against certain colors before I print the image and buy a mat for the frame. Elements can do this for you although it's largely an undocumented trick. The background of an image window can be filled by using the Paint Bucket tool, using any foreground color.

1. Double-click the Hand tool and then drag the image window away from the image so you can see the gray background.

2. Choose any color you like by clicking the foreground color swatch and then choosing your color from the Color Picker.

3. Choose the Paint Bucket tool and then Shift+click over the window background.

   You can see the results here.

4. To undo the effect (every image you open will now have this background color), click the foreground color swatch.

5. In the Color Picker, select the B radio button in the HSB field, type 50 in the B percentage field, and then press Enter.

6. Shift+click over the image background with the Paint Bucket.

From an editing point of view, it's usually best to work against a 50% black background, but now you know how to do something a lot of Photoshop users are unaware of.

Img2003-07-06_160802.JPG @ 25% (RGB/8*)

25%   0.7s

Wiley, the Wiley Publishing logo, For Dummies, the Dummies Man logo, the For Dummies Bestselling Book Series logo and all related trade dress are trademarks or registered trademarks of John Wiley & Sons, Inc. and/or its affiliates. All other trademarks are property of their respective owners.

For Dummies: Bestselling Book Series for Beginners

Photoshop® Elements

ALL-IN-ONE DESK REFERENCE

FOR DUMMIES®

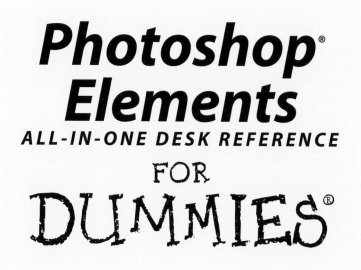

Photoshop® Elements
ALL-IN-ONE DESK REFERENCE
FOR DUMMIES®

Gary David Bouton

Wiley Publishing, Inc.

Photoshop® Elements All-in-One Desk Reference For Dummies®

Published by
Wiley Publishing, Inc.
111 River Street
Hoboken, NJ 07030-5774
www.wiley.com

Copyright © 2006 by Wiley Publishing, Inc., Indianapolis, Indiana

Published by Wiley Publishing, Inc., Indianapolis, Indiana

Published simultaneously in Canada

WILEY

About the Author

Gary David Bouton has written 21 books on computer graphics, 13 of them on Photoshop, several of which have won the John Newbery Medal — and that's the only lie in this book. A professional illustrator, Gary has won four international awards for graphics and Desktop Publishing, and hosts the Application Convergence forum at Photoshop Gurus (www.photoshopgurus.com/forum/index.php?board=13.0). It's a place that'll remind you of this book, where the author will gladly answer questions you might have after reading any of his work. Gary lives in a secluded hamlet in upstate New York where in his spare time, he enjoys playing the Elements installation CD on the home stereo, teaching his cat Norris how to drive a stick shift, and asking for the kids' menu at Friendly's just so he can color in the clowns and dinosaurs.

Dedication

This one is for my mother, Eileen. She is a constant source of inspiration, and has been a terrific sounding board and confidant all my years. Thanks, Mom.

Author's Acknowledgments

I need to thank my agent Matt Wagner for hooking me up with the fine people at Wiley. Thanks to acquisitions editor Bob Woerner for everything and project editor Pat O'Brien for his hand-holding and sage council throughout the manuscript reviews. Also a hearty thanks and salutation to copy editor Teresa Artman for adding parallelism, repairing gerunds, and fixing several other literary offenses that I am prone to committing. A tip o' the hat to Composition Services for laying out the splendid color book you hold before you. Also, thanks to Charat Maheshwari, Mark Dahm, and the other brilliant and diligent people at Adobe Systems, without which there would be no Elements 4, and therefore no *For Dummies* book. Special thanks to Kate Moir at Xara, Ltd., for Xara Xtreme, used extensively in this book for figure annotations and original art.

Thanks to my buddies Gordon Robinson, Mara Zebest, Maya Doku, Gary Eden, Carol DeSalvo, and my wife Barbara for permission to use their fine photography in this book. Equal thanks go to Surya, my brother Dave, Matt, Julian Berman, Bob, and others who agreed to pose for the camera for often extremely silly stuff.

Publisher's Acknowledgments

We're proud of this book; please send us your comments through our online registration form located at `www.dummies.com/register/`.

Some of the people who helped bring this book to market include the following:

Acquisitions, Editorial, and Media Development

Senior Project Editor: Pat O'Brien

Senior Acquisitions Editor: Bob Woerner

Senior Copy Editor: Teresa Artman

Technical Editor: Bill Moorehead

Editorial Manager: Kevin Kirschner

Media Development Specialists: Angela Denny, Kate Jenkins, Steven Kudirka, Kit Malone, Travis Silvers

Media Development Coordinator: Laura Atkinson

Media Project Supervisor: Laura Moss

Media Development Manager: Laura VanWinkle

Editorial Assistant: Amanda Foxworth

Cartoons: Rich Tennant (`www.the5thwave.com`)

Composition Services

Project Coordinator: Erin Smith

Layout and Graphics: Lauren Goddard, Denny Hager, LeAndra Hosier, Lynsey Osborn, Melanee Prendergast, Heather Ryan

Proofreaders: Laura L. Bowman, Jessica Kramer

Indexer: Valerie Haynes Perry

Special Help: Kim Darosett, Andy Hollandbeck, Becky Huehls, Blair Pottenger, Virginia Sanders, Rebecca Senninger, Nicole Sholly, Becky Whitney

Publishing and Editorial for Technology Dummies

    Richard Swadley, Vice President and Executive Group Publisher

    Andy Cummings, Vice President and Publisher

    Mary Bednarek, Executive Acquisitions Director

    Mary C. Corder, Editorial Director

Publishing for Consumer Dummies

    Diane Graves Steele, Vice President and Publisher

    Joyce Pepple, Acquisitions Director

Composition Services

    Gerry Fahey, Vice President of Production Services

    Debbie Stailey, Director of Composition Services

Contents at a Glance

Table of Contents

Introduction

Hello and welcome to *Photoshop Elements All-in-One Desk Reference For Dummies,* which is also a terrific step-by-step guide (but that wouldn't fit on the cover). This book takes you through techniques, workarounds, and less-than-obvious features of Elements, and also provides you with all the elements you need to become familiar with Adobe Elements. As a reference book, you can quickly sift through the information at hand to find the nugget of wisdom you need at the moment so that you can spend the rest of your time doing the things you bought Elements for: making your photos look better, doing really cool stuff with photos (like you see in print ads and supermarket magazines), and more.

If you're just getting into digital photography and retouching, this book will satisfy your need to know stuff as the occasion arises. For example, as a newcomer, you need to know how to configure Elements to obey your beck and call as well as several other things, naturally: correcting photo color and exposure, creating and navigating image layers, selecting image areas, cloning, painting, erasing, filtering, and following good composition guidelines.

If you already own image-retouching and -editing books so huge that they'd fracture your toes if you dropped them, you might very well be overwhelmed by the amount of detail and mutter to yourself, "Do I *really* need to read 1,432.3 pages about color gamuts and lighting ratios to fix my wedding photos?", or "Do I really need a book that dwarfs the *Physician's Desktop Reference* to show me how to separate a background from my mother-in-law?" The truth is that many extremely thick and dense Photoshop books have a few pages of really useful information — the kind you use every day — and the rest consist of details bordering on obsession that apply mostly to trivia buffs and statistics freaks.

This book is a distillation of what you want to know, and it's ready to go when you want to know. The concept behind this book is to take all the useful Elements information and put it in context so it's meaningful and relevant in your explorations. Whether you're a novice or pro, Elements 4 is new to everyone, so you've found the right book.

About Photoshop Elements

I've occasionally been asked, "Is Elements like Photoshop CS, or is it just a kiddie version?" To make a comparison, Elements is to Photoshop what a large slice of really good cake is to the whole cake. There are a few features in Photoshop that weren't brought into Elements, but the features that were brought in are every bit as powerful as those in Photoshop. Some features are hidden (I show you how to reveal them), and Elements actually offers a number of tools not available in Photoshop. Plus, many procedures are menued in a wizard-like fashion, so you can accomplish tedious tasks with only a click or two. Throughout this book, I refer to Elements as simply *Elements,* with the occasional reference to Photoshop CS as simply *Photoshop* to avoid confusion.

About This Book

This book doesn't pretend to be a comprehensive reference for every detail of the interface; instead, it shows you how to get up and running fast so that you have more time to do the things you really want to do. Designed by using the easy-to-follow *For Dummies* format, this book helps you get the information you need without laboring to find it.

Photoshop Elements All-in-One Desk Reference For Dummies is a big book made up of several smaller books. Each mini-book covers the basics of one key aspect of Elements, such as color correction, selecting image areas, and the other application modules in the Elements suite. Whenever one big thing is made up of several smaller things, confusion is always a possibility. That's why this book is designed to branch out like a tree. At the very beginning is a detailed Table of Contents that covers the entire book. Then, each mini-book begins with an outline of contents that shows you at a glance what's covered in that mini-book. Useful running heads appear at the top of each page to point out the topic discussed on that page. And handy thumbtabs run down the side of the pages to help you quickly find each book. Finally, a lush, comprehensive index enables you to find information anywhere in the entire book.

Although it's a reference book, it also has a logical flow: You can choose to pick it up when you're stuck or read it in sequence in front of a crackling fireplace with a cup of cocoa and your golden retriever at your feet. You can begin at the beginning, discovering how to install, optimize, and customize Elements, and then move on to simple and then more challenging techniques. Everything you need to do to accomplish different types of image editing is mapped out with example images in clear, easy-to-follow steps. But this book is mostly a handy, indispensable guide: the kind of book you can pick up, turn to just about any page, and discover possibilities.

You can find all sample files that I use in this book at www.dummies.com/ go/PhotoshopElementsAIOFD1e.

How to Use This Book

Open it. Start with the topic you want to find out about. Look for the topic in the Table of Contents or in the index to get going. The Table of Contents is detailed enough that you should be able to find most of the topics you're looking for. If not, turn to the index, where you can find even more detail.

If you want to take a brief excursion into a topic, by all means go for it. If you want to look at the big picture on typography, read the whole chapter on typography. If you just want to know how to use the Type tools, read just that chapter. You get the idea.

Whenever I describe a message or information that you see onscreen, I present it as follows:

```
Elements is unhappy and needs to restart
```

If you need to type something, you see the text you need to type in bold: **You could already be a winner**. In this example, you type **You could already be a winner** and then press Enter. When it isn't obvious why I ask you to type something, an explanation usually follows.

How This Book Is Organized

Each of the nine mini-books contained in *Photoshop Elements All-in-One Desk Reference For Dummies* can stand alone. The first book covers installation, Elements preference, and a basic voyage into the suite's modules. I won't presume a thing about your level of experience with Windows or Elements, so if you're an old hand (or even a middle-aged hand) at either, you might want to skim over Book I quickly for laughs. The remaining books cover a variety of imaging and graphics topics that you would normally find covered in separate, costly, and humorless books. Here's a brief description of what you find in each book.

Book I: Getting Started

This mini-book covers installation; Elements preferences (do *not* gloss over preferences — they're critical to Elements performance and your own sanity); Quick Fix; and Organizer and the other modules. Here I give you a guide to commands, tools, palettes, and shortcuts. You can find steps for creating custom brush tips, creating your own gradient fills, and replacing colors in an image.

The Cheat Sheet at the front of the book is full of shortcut keys.

Book II: Acquiring Images

In this mini-book, you become acquainted with the various ways to get images and artwork into your computer and into Elements — after all, Elements is an editor and not a photo-creation application. From digital cameras to Photo CDs made from 35mm film, from scanning photos to using different graphics programs to generate photorealistic backgrounds, it's all laid out in Book II.

Book III: Color Correction

The unwanted tints in photos are a big problem. You know, when an indoor photo casts red or when an outdoor photograph casts blue. Book III shows how to correct the colors in a picture by using both Quick Fix and manual techniques, how to adjust image exposure to get crisp whites and deep rich shadows, and how to unadjust color to create a vintage photo and other fascinating, provocative imagery.

Book IV: Creating and Using Selections

Many average photos need only part of the picture modified. In Book IV, you gain experience with the Elements selection tools so that you can isolate and then correct or enhance image areas. You can drag and even paint on selections, and then you can modify the selection by distorting it, adding to it, or removing from a selection.

Book V: Working with Layers

Layers provide the easiest and quickest way to make image areas from different pictures into a full-blown composition. Book V submerges you in the depths of multiple layers, showing you how to get a selection onto a layer, duplicate and hide layers, merge layers, and use layer blending mode — think of this as Layers Meet Abbott & Costello.

Book VI: Basic Image Retouching

This mini-book covers the restoration and enhancement of images that have minor flaws in the composition. Fixing red-eye, straightening a photo, and sharpening/blurring image areas are all examined. Photo restoration — making an image that's been lying around in a shoebox since 1953 look like new — is also featured in detail.

Book VII: Typing the Text

Covered in this mini-book is not only how to create paragraph and normal (display) text but also good typography rules. You find out about text justification, line spacing, text warping, and special effects. You see how to copy text into Elements, add extended characters such as fractions and curly quotes, and apply text as a selection marquee ready for special fills.

Book VIII: Ambitious Image Retouching

Discover here how to replace backgrounds in images, add or remove folks from family photos, create shadows and haloes, clone people without using stem cells, and more. Repair the impossible and create the unreal.

Book IX: Creating Special-Effects Images

With this trusty mini-book at your side, you can create fantasy images such as an invisible man, a centaur, floating elephants, toys as large as houses, neon text, and other imagination-stretchers. Also, find out about undocumented, hidden Elements features (such as the invaluable Masking Layer) as well as how to build your own ready-to-print digital scrapbook better than if you used a template.

Bonus Web Chapters: Outputting for the Screen

There's more Photoshop Elements goodness on our Web site. Bonus chapters on the Web site cover the things you need to know to print to an inkjet or other printer: image resolution, color modes, and some tricks for making outstanding prints. Additionally, I discuss outputting to 35mm slides at a service bureau and ordering prints online from wallet size to poster size. As a bonus, you can also find info on creating GIF animations for the Web, writing a slide show of your work to CD with transitions and text so you and others can watch it on TV, and using Elements to create a Web gallery.

Icons Used in This Book

Like any *For Dummies* book, this book is chock-full of helpful icons that draw your attention to items of particular importance. You find the following icons throughout this book:

Hold it — technical stuff is just around the corner. Read on only if you display nerdy qualities and frequently use the word *paradigm* correctly.

Pay special attention to this icon; it tunes you into useful information that lies outside of reference material.

These paragraphs contain tips that are better stored in your head than in the book, for even quicker reference. Do you remember Question Mark & The Mysterians, Gobi boots, and when Tiny Tim married Miss Vickie on Carson? If not, that's okay; I'm just being nostalgic here.

This icon highlights information that might help you avert disaster, such as when Elements is running low on resources; when you've made more than three editing mistakes (*hint:* choose Window⇨Undo History); and when you're spending too much time with your computer and not enough with your family.

Software Used for Figures in This Book

My experience has been that computer graphics software is mix and match: A lot of times you need to tap into the individual strengths of a number of applications to arrive at a finished, cohesive body of work. If you wonder about some of the figures in this book and online (www.dummies.com/go/PhotoshopElementsAIOFD1e), that's great — it was my intention. If you're wondering how they were done, that shouldn't be a secret. Here's what I used:

+ I used **Xara Xtreme** to edit, annotate, and enhance most of the screen figures.

+ I used **Photoshop CS2** — but just a little — for image enhancement because this is a book on Elements and I didn't want to cheat.

+ I used many different modeling programs to create synthetic images to illustrate camera angles and other 3-D objects. I used **Poser, Vue d'Esprit,** and **trueSpace** the most frequently.

+ I created textures by using **DarkTree** and other applications outside of Elements.

+ I used **FontLab** to create the original typefaces, and fonts used in the figures came from **URW, Émigré,** and **ITC.**

Where to Go from Here

Just roll the dice and move your playing piece an equal amount of spaces. Seriously, with this book in hand, you're all set to conquer pixels and make your mark in the world as a Fellow Photoshoppist. Browse the Table of Contents and decide where you want to start. Take charge, take heart, and take five when you're exhausted. And most of all, have as much fun getting to know Elements as I did writing this book.

Book I
Getting Started

*N*o more stalling — the time has come to install Elements. In this mini-book, I help you set up your Elements preferences, which are critical to Elements performance and your own sanity. You also discover how to make Quick Fix, Organizer, and the other modules behave according to your desires. Here, I give you a guide to commands, tools, palettes, and shortcuts. If you're longing to create custom brush tips, design your own gradient fills, and replace colors in an image, well then, you're in the right mini-book.

Chapter 1: To Begin at the Beginning

In This Chapter

- ✓ Installing Photoshop Elements
- ✓ Examining the different modules
- ✓ Organizing files
- ✓ Quick fixing images
- ✓ File formats and options

It's a fair guess that you bought Photoshop Elements because it was recommended by someone whose opinion you value, or you've seen a friend working in Photoshop and said, "*Expletive! I* want a piece of that, but I want a more user-friendly version."

The good news is that you made the right choice because Photoshop Elements is the best image editing program you can get for the price. The not-so-good news is that like anything worthwhile, Elements expertise requires that you somewhat diligently become familiar with its features. (We all know that buying an exercycle and keeping it in the basement doesn't by itself guarantee weight loss.) And it would be a shame to shun learning and using every penny's worth of Elements' power because investing some quality time (ahem, turn off the TV) can provide you with the know-how to do some unbelievable restoration and special effects with your photos.

Photoshop Elements All-In-One Desk Reference For Dummies is also a good purchase because here I guide you through all the steps you need to arrive at a collection of digital images that are breathtaking. But you gotta start someplace, and installation of Elements seems like a good diving-in point.

You can purchase Photoshop Elements 4 for Windows at www.adobe.com ($99 US for an installation CD, and $79 US to upgrade from version 3). Version 4 is available for Windows and Macintosh, but Macintosh users can't use the Organizer and Create modules (unless they run Elements under Windows emulation).

If you're running version 3, Mac or Windows, you can use this book to find out about all but the new tools, the commands, the palettes, and all the other good stuff except for the Elements sister modules. The Organizer and Create modules are exclusive to version 4.

Setting Up Elements

I won't assume that you've already installed Elements (although this assumption flies in the face of how I buy and install software — like a child opening a birthday present with abandon and glee — don't we all do this?). You want to do two things to make your life (and work) in Elements more pleasant: Load it where you have the most hard drive space and then choose your file import filters.

Checking your free drive space before you install Elements

Elements needs about 275MB of free space on your hard drive. By default, Elements and most other programs want to install in the `C:\Program Files` folder. This is not a good idea for two reasons:

✦ **Bloat:** If you let every application install to your C: drive, you soon run out of space on that hard drive. If you have only one hard drive and don't have partitions (such as D:, E:, and so on), of course you must install Elements to C:. (In the following step list, I show you how to discern whether you have more than one drive partitioned.)

✦ **Safety:** It's not wise to install programs to the same drive as your operating system because an error written by Elements can affect various parts of your whole C: partition, including your operating system. (Errors sometimes create cross-linked hard drive clusters.) However, if your PC is set up with multiple drives and/or partitions, you can instruct Elements to install on a different drive — ideally, a drive that has a lot of free space.

To decide which hard drive or partition is the best one on which to install Elements, follow these steps:

1. **Double-click My Computer on the desktop.**

2. **Choose View⇨Details.**

   This changes the view in the My Computer window to show all the important details about the drives on your computer.

3. **Look at the last number next to all the drives — the Free Space amount — and note which drive or partition has the most free space.**

Your target is 300MB of free space, a rounded-up value, to be on the safe side.

This is the hard drive on which you should install Photoshop Elements. In Figure 1-1, you can see that the F: drive has the most space.

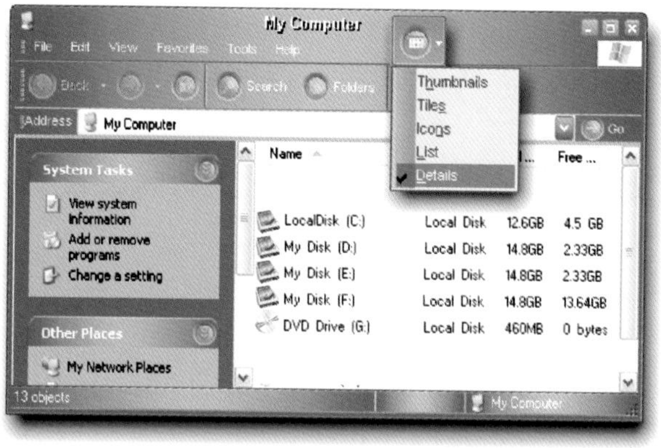

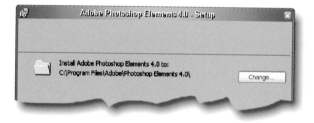

Figure 1-1: Check which drive has the largest amount of free space.

Time to install:

1. **Insert the Elements CD and begin the installation, following the prompts and directions. If you downloaded the installation program, double-click the InstallShield icon in the folder.**

2. **When you come to the installation screen that asks you where you want Elements, follow these steps to change the default setting:**

   a. *Click the Change button (see Figure 1-2).*

   b. *Choose the hard drive or partition with the largest amount of free space.*

Figure 1-2: Install Elements where you have plenty of room.

Choosing file import filters

Elements can open just about any bitmap file format (and vector designs, covered later in this book), but you need to specify which file types you want, or (big sigh here) you need to uninstall and reinstall Elements. In Figure 1-3, you can see the Setup screen where you choose which filters you want.

You don't need all the filters. Table 1-1 lists the file formats that you'll use 99 percent of your time in Elements. Understandably, if you omit one of these file formats, Elements won't be able to open that file type.

Table 1-1	File Formats You Want to Choose
Type of File	*File Extension*
Adobe Photoshop Document	PSD
Windows Bitmap	BMP
Digital Negative	DNG
CompuServe	GIF
JPEG	JPG, JPEG
PC Exchange	PCX
Portable Document Format	PDF
Portable Network Graphics	PNG
Photoshop Raw	RAW
Targa	TGA
Tagged Image File Format	TIF
Encapsulated PostScript	EPS, AI, PS

Don't mistake this Setup dialog box for *file associations* (the file types that are identified by filename suffixes, such as .bmp). You set up which application opens what type of bitmap in Elements by either

✦ Choosing Edit⇨File Association in Elements

or

✦ Choosing Tools⇨Folder Options in a Windows drive window and then clicking the File Types tab

That's about it for installing Elements. After you click Finish, the Elements icon appears on the desktop, under Start⇨All Programs. Appropriately enough, this icon is a tiny, silver camera.

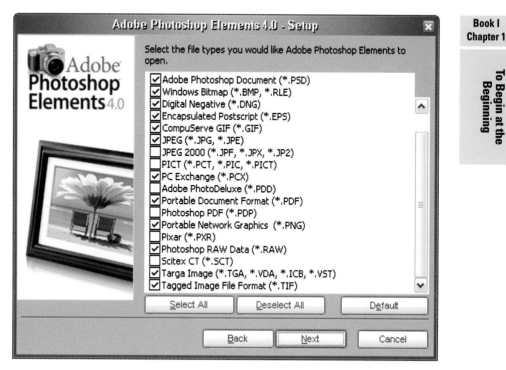

Figure 1-3: Choose file formats here that you want to open in Elements.

By allowing Elements to import many file formats, you're assured that graphics created by using programs other than Elements can be imported, cataloged, edited, and saved to different formats. However, you need only about six different file formats for exporting Elements work, and I cover them at the end of this chapter.

Setting profiles via Adobe Gamma Loader

Elements automatically installs the *Adobe Gamma Loader* utility to your Control Panel (accessible by choosing Start➪Settings➪Control Panel). This utility corrects color casting that your monitor might display.

Newer LCD (liquid crystal diode) monitors might not even need *calibration,* which is the adjustment of white point, black point, midrange breadth (gamma), and color temperature (color casting).

Your finished calibration affects all programs that use ICC (International Color Consortium, the folks who set the standards) profiles, which include all Adobe applications and many other graphics programs but not *every* application you might own. A *profile* is a set of commands in a text file that tells the application how to save and display an image; the term is synonymous with *color profile,* a term that Elements and Photoshop CS use.

Loading settings and calibrating your monitor by using the Adobe Gamma Loader is painless; just follow these steps:

1. **Open the Control Panel (choose Start➪Settings➪Control Panel); in the Control Panel, double-click Adobe Gamma.**

2. **Choose Step By Step Wizard and then click the Next button.**

3. **In the Description text box, type a name for the profile.**

   Use a name that you can remember easily, such as 07-14-2006. When you save the monitor calibration at the end of the wizard, you type the same name.

4. **Click Next and follow the instructions.**

   Before you save the settings, click the Before and After buttons to see how the changes you made affect the monitor's display. Adjust the color and tone of the display by choosing from the menu boxes. The dialog box interactively refreshes your monitor display, so what you see is what you get.

After you create the ICC profile, Gamma Loader saves it in the `Windows/System32/Spool/Drivers/Color` folder, but you shouldn't ever need to delete or move this file. Gamma Loader is a "set it, then forget it" utility.

Starting Photoshop Elements

You're in for a (pleasant) surprise after you double-click the Elements icon to open Elements for the first time. Elements comprises four modules, and the Welcome screen opens to the module in which you want to work. If you want, you can have all the modules open albeit at the peril of a system stress-out.

As you can see in Figure 1-4, you can use the modules to do the following:

✦ **View and Organize Photos:** The Organizer module enables you to, well, view and organize your photos, just like the icon says.

✦ **Quickly Fix Photos:** The Quick Fix module makes it easy to make simple adjustments to your photos. You can sharpen, brighten, and correct color cast, but you don't have any real editing tools in this module.

✦ **Edit and Enhance Photos:** The Editor module is the main module that I call Elements. Here, you can do the real work of editing your photos.

✦ **Make Photo Creations:** The Create module enables you to use your photos to make a presentation or scrapbook.

You don't edit photos in the Create module.

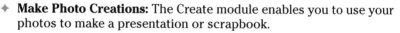

Key modules

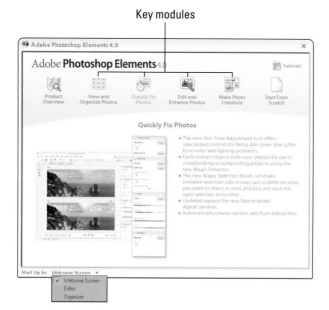

Figure 1-4: Choose your work module from the Welcome screen.

To go straight to the Editor module, which is the main topic of this book, I suggest that you select the Editor check box at the bottom of the Welcome screen. Then you'll go straight to the Editor the next time you launch Elements, which saves time when you load Elements. You can always get back to the Welcome screen from within the Editor by choosing Window⇨Welcome Screen (see Figure 1-5).

Figure 1-5: Choose how Elements welcomes you.

The Organizer Module

The Organizer module is where the action begins if you're not ready to try your hand at image editing. If you want to create a presentation or a calendar, go to the Organizer module by clicking the View and Organize Photos icon in the Welcome screen; if you're in the Editor module, go to the Organizer module by clicking the Photo Browser (why the two different names eludes me) button, just above the Options bar.

For example, gathering image files (and music; Organizer can catalog tunes and movies, too) in Organizer gives you a handy, efficient thumbnail view of your work. If you're like me, organizing my user files ranks on my priority list right after answering spam.

Assuming that you just installed Elements, you don't yet have a *collection* — a subset of the catalog — which is actually a bunch of tags, referring to the catalog. Organizer is a storage box; it doesn't do the sorting for you.

You begin with filling the catalog. Having your images stored in a special folder on your hard drive makes building the catalog easier. If your images aren't all contained in one folder, though, that's cool — it just means a little more work.

To add images to your catalog, follow these steps:

 1. **Click the camera icon and choose From Files and Folders from the menu that appears, as shown in Figure 1-6.**

   You get a directory dialog box, where you choose the path to your photo stash.

Figure 1-6: Add images from here.

2. **To add a whole folder of images, click the folder icon and then click the Get Photos button.**

If you want only some of the images in a hard drive folder included in your catalog, open a folder, press Ctrl+A (to select all), and then hold Ctrl and click the image filenames that you don't want in the catalog.

3. **Clear the Automatically Fix Red Eyes check box — because it's better to edit a photo with this flaw in the Editor module — and then click OK, as shown in Figure 1-7.**

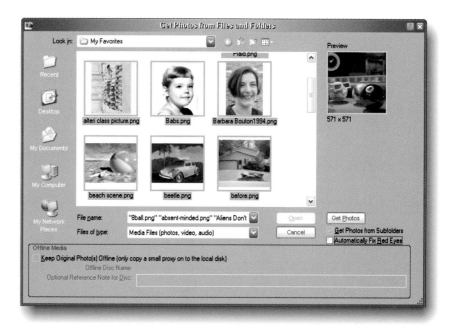

Figure 1-7: Organizer collects images by filename and displays thumbnails as you catalog.

You're on the right track but not quite done. You've done coarse cataloging, but a catalog isn't a collection. And if all the photos you want included aren't in one single folder, repeat the preceding steps.

If you're a drag-and-drop sort of PC user, here's a good way to add images to your catalog:

1. **Minimize the Organizer (by clicking the Minimize/Restore button in the upper-right corner of the Elements window).**

2. **Open a file folder from My Computer on your desktop.**

3. **Drag image files into Organizer's catalog view.**

From catalog to collection in Organizer

A *collection* is a subset of the catalog; a collection is actually a bunch of tags, referring to the catalog. Collections make it a joy to browse only those images within a specific collection; there's no sifting to do. Begin a collection like this:

1. **Choose New⇨New Collection.**

   You're immediately presented with a dialog box that wants to know what image you want to use as your collection icon. Because you chose a number of file format options in setup, all your TIF, BMP, and other images show up in this box.

2. **In the Create Collection dialog box, click the Edit Icon button and then pick an image.**

   Organizer copies, shrinks, and crops the image. You can delete the source image at any time afterward.

3. **Name the collection.**

4. **Optionally, make any notes that will help you remember what images are stored in this collection. See Figure 1-8.**

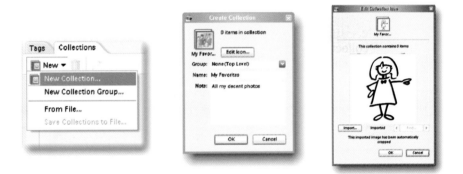

Figure 1-8: Start a collection by naming it.

Elements ships with *tags* (which are similar to collections), such as Family and Wedding. You can use these tags by dragging the tag on top of images, but you can also create collections with the same names — Organizer will display an attention box that says certain images may be too small to print, but you can safely dismiss it. "Hey, Elements! Maybe I don't want to print my whole catalog. Instead, I want to view it onscreen" is also a fair reply.

After creating a collection, it's time to populate your collection. Just drag your collection title on top of an image in the main catalog window, as shown in Figure 1-9. A tiny icon of the image you defined for a specific catalog appears next to images you've tagged.

Figure 1-9: Build a collection by dragging its title to a catalog thumbnail.

It really doesn't get simpler. And if you want an image to be in more than one collection, you drag the additional collection tag on top of the same image in the catalog window.

You can't reorder image thumbnails in the catalog, but you can reorder with any view of your collections — just drag and drop a thumbnail to reposition it. This is very important because thumbnail order determines the order in which images appear in the Create module compositions.

Basic editing in Organizer

Although the Editor is the place to be with your images when photos need medium-to-major repair, you can rely on Organizer to perform a few minor corrections.

For example, in Figure 1-10, you can see a scanned image that had to be sampled sideways. Without the need for the Editor, you can change such an image to upright it by clicking the Rotate Right or the Rotate Left icon, as shown in the figure.

Figure 1-10: Organizer offers several ways in which you can view your collection.

A warning box appears (see Figure 1-11), telling you that the image is not the correct format for rotation without compromising the original image data, and offering to rotate a copy of the image. Only PSD and TIFF image formats can be rotated losslessly — and these image files can't have layers. *Lossless* means that no image data is converted when you rotate an image or perform other edits. Layers are covered throughout Book V; they're instrumental to creating sophisticated imagery.

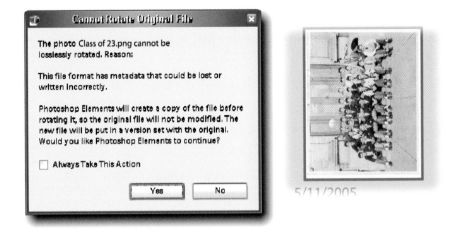

Figure 1-11: Elements plans to copy your file before rotating it.

View options at the bottom of the Organizer module interface (refer to Figure 1-10) enable you to zoom the page, view only a selected image, or see a full-screen slide show.

You can do a slide show in any folder window in Windows at any time.

Adding file info in Organizer

The date on which a photo was taken obviously doesn't tell you much. To compensate for this, Organizer enables you to caption thumbnails. Here's how:

1. **Double-click a thumbnail to move to the individual viewing pane.**

2. **Click in the caption area and type a comment.**

3. **When you're done, click the Back to All Photos button.**

4. **(Optional) To add more information, press Alt+Enter.**

   For example, in the Properties box, you can add notes, edit your comment field, and get the file location, date, and file size. See Figure 1-12.

Figure 1-12: Add info and get the lowdown on photos in your collection.

The Quick Fix Mode

Quick Fix is not so much a unique Elements module but rather a mode of the Elements Editor module. Use Quick Fix mode on those occasions when a photo's defects are too baffling to address in standard Edit mode (what most folks simply call *Elements*), or if you just want to make, well, a quick fix to a photo. In Quick Fix mode, most editing tools and commands are unavailable, but color and tone correcting are at hand, as is sharpening.

You can certainly perform all these tasks better by using more advanced features, which I cover throughout this book. However, when you only need to crop, resize, or color-correct a photo, Quick Fix can do in a pinch.

Here's an example you can follow to perform a little image enhancement using Quick Fix:

1. **Choose an image of your own that needs sprucing up.**

2. **Click the Quick Fix button under Elements Editor's main menu.**

3. **Choose Before and After View from the drop-down menu at the bottom of the interface.**

4. **Choose the orientation of your image:**

   • **Portrait:** If your image is tall

   • **Landscape:** If your image is wide

   Your tool set is very limited in Quick Fix mode because Quick Fix is used only for adjusting an image's colors — not for painting. (You can select an image area for adjusting before you go to Quick Fix.)

5. **Adjust the image by dragging or clicking the Color sliders and buttons until the image looks markedly better. Here's what the controls do:**

   • **Temperature** (see Figure 1-13) controls the blue-to-red color cast in an image. Left casts cool; and right, warm.

   • **Tint** determines the green-to-magenta color cast, as you can see in Figure 1-14.

   • **Auto buttons** are the "no-brainer" controls; you click them, and they automatically fix tone and color. You have no artistic control when you click Auto, and because you're more intelligent than a software program, you usually get better results if you drag the sliders instead.

   • The **Reset button** (above the After image pane in the upcoming Figure 1-15) works only if you first click an Auto button.

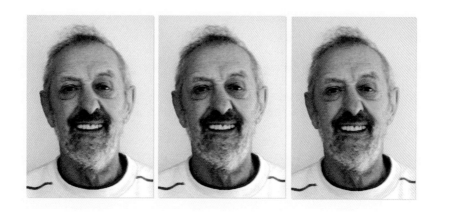

Figure 1-13: Quickly tweak temperature here.

In Quick Fix mode, you cannot undo a slider's results except by fiddling with it more and then judging the change by eye. Argh factor: This remedy is wildly inaccurate because the sliders don't have tick marks. To truly undo a slider change, switch back to Standard Edit mode and then press Ctrl+Z.

Original   More green (better)   More magenta (wrong)

Figure 1-14: Quickly tweak tint here.

In Figure 1-15, I clicked the Quick Fix button. The image's background, which was dulled through a glass pane when the photograph was taken with a flash, is lightened — as is the boy's hair — without messing much with the skin tones or other colors. Try this on flash photography photos with dull — or apparently missing — backgrounds.

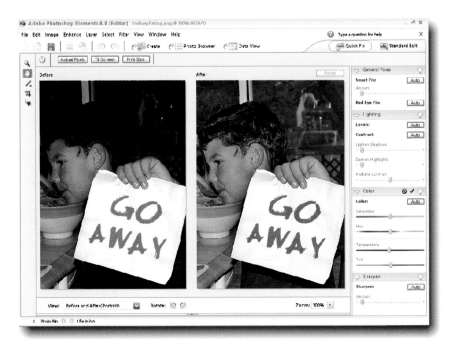

Figure 1-15: Quick Fix might be all you need to correct images that are more "snapshot" than fine photography.

The Create Module

When you want to create a scrapbook or a slide show, clicking the Create button below the main menu takes you to the Organizer, where you choose the collection from which the Create module does its thing; then you click Create again.

The Create module (see Figure 1-16) is your one-stop shop for letting Elements build you a sophisticated slide show (with zooms, transitions, and even music), greeting cards, customized calendars . . . you name it.

If you want to get going right now, however, go ahead: The menu system in the Create module is pretty goof-proof, but note that creations for print require high-resolution images. You might get a warning message telling you that an image's resolution is too small to print well — those images are marked with a tiny exclamation point/road sign icon, as shown in Figure 1-17. My advice is to continue because you likely don't have the same image in a larger resolution — or else you would've put it in your collection.

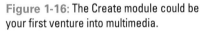

Figure 1-16: The Create module could be your first venture into multimedia.

Figure 1-17: When Elements squawks about low resolution, forge ahead.

The Date View

Date View is part of the Editor module, and a way to view your photo collection by the date the photos were taken or last modified. You do see your photos on a calendar, but Date View isn't like the Calendar option in the Create module. Rather, Date View is sort of a personal calendar that you can annotate. Images taken on a specific day appear on the calendar, one at a time.

♦ To scroll through the images taken on a given day, navigate via the VCR-like controls at the top right.

♦ To change the date on a thumbnail as it appears on the Date View calendar, follow these steps:

1. Double-click the day.

2. Choose the alternative image.

3. Click Month view at the bottom of the interface. Figure 1-18 shows the Create New dialog box that you get when you right-click a date.

If you've taken more than one photo on a particular day, the VCR controls light up in the upper-right corner of the interface and you can advance and go back to preview all the pictures.

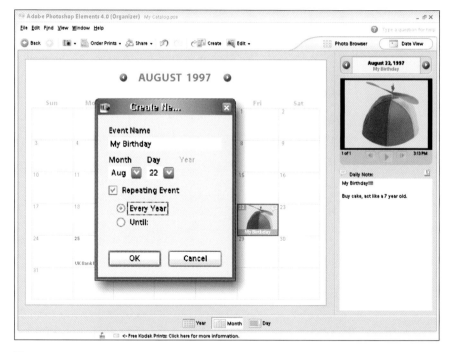

Figure 1-18: Right-click a date to work with this dialog box.

As visually interesting as Date View is, it's not a full-featured calendar program, so don't try to use it to keep your schedule organized. Although Date View in Elements provides you with a notes field, the Microsoft Outlook Calendar is a better scheduling tool:

✦ Outlook provides more scheduling capabilities (including a notes field, alarms, and to-do lists).

✦ Outlook uses fewer system resources and loads faster.

If you're already in Organizer, there's no reason not to use Date View, and of course it's a graphically rich little applet. But my list of cons outweighs the pros. In a nutshell, Date View is free, fun to use, and unnecessary.

Saving Your Images

Eventually, sooner rather than later, you need to save your work. Although Elements can save to many different file formats, these six will suit 99 percent of your needs (presented roughly in order of popularity):

✦ **PSD:** The native file format for Photoshop CS and Elements

✦ **TIFF:** Tagged Image File Format, sometimes abbreviated as TIF

✦ **JPEG:** Joint Photographers Experts Group, sometimes abbreviated as JPG

✦ **PNG:** Portable Network Graphics, a free and open standard

✦ **GIF:** Graphics Interchange Format, owned by CompuServe

✦ **BMP:** Microsoft Windows native file format

If you're in a time crunch, choose PSD (Photoshop's native file format). PSD is the only format that can save all the Elements editing you do in an image, such as layers, layer styles, text as editable text, saved selections, and other data that's proprietary to Elements.

In the following sections, I describe these save file formats in order of frequency of use.

PSD options

As you pore through this book, you'll discover that you can add many special things to a photo composition: text, vector shapes, layers, transparency, and styles, to name a few. Elements can write a composite photo to formats other than PSD, but text saved to another format (BMP, for example) loses its editability, and layers flatten to a single layer. Layers are an indispensable editing feature, much like shuffling photo clippings up or down in a stack to make an overlapping collage; they're covered extensively in Book V.

Although only PSD and TIFF can save layers, don't worry. Elements warns you in advance that these changes will happen if you save the file in another format.

In Figure 1-19, you can see the Save As dialog box; I'm trying to save a layered image to BMP format. Elements — if I continue — will flatten the file. The only reason to save to BMP is to use such a saved file as Windows desktop wallpaper — it's not a very robust, options-filled image format.

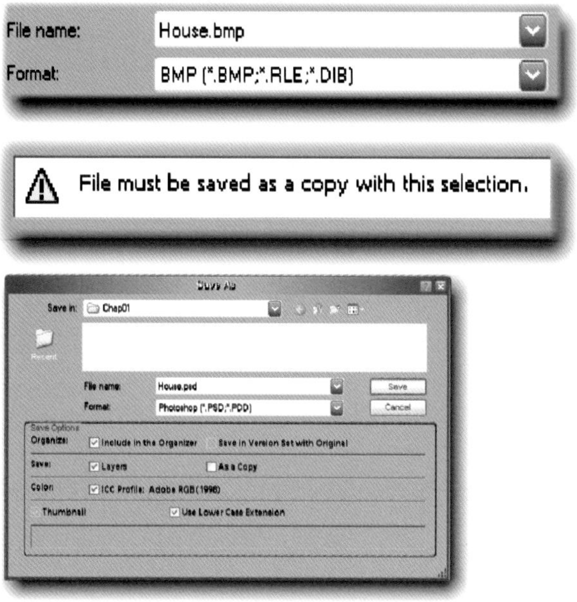

Figure 1-19: Only PSD and TIFF can save layers.

However, when you save to PSD file format, everything is preserved and editable in future Elements sessions. Take a look at these check boxes in the Save As dialog box (as shown in Figure 1-19) that need investigating:

✦ **Include in the Organizer:** When this is marked, Elements automatically saves a thumbnail and the file's path on your hard drive. However, you then need to include it in a collection from the catalog. (Read more about the Organizer, collections, and catalogs earlier in this chapter.)

✦ **Layers:** When this is selected, layers are preserved.

By all means, save layers!

✦ **ICC Profile:** *ICC profiles* are color spaces into which the image is fit. Adobe RGB (1998) is the largest, and therefore the best profile for your valuable images.

If an sRGB check box appears, follow these steps to save yourself the mistake of saving a file to this unwanted profile:

1. *Cancel out of Save.*

2. *Choose Edit⇨Color Settings.*

3. *Click the Optimize for Printing button.*

4. *Press Ctrl+S.*

✦ **As a Copy:** Read more about this option in the upcoming section, "PNG file format." You're saving a copy of the image and it remains unchanged in the workspace.

✦ **Maximize Compatibility:** Okay, this check box isn't on the Save As dialog box, but you might come across it after you make your choices from the preceding options and then click Save.

Photoshop has new features with every version (such as Shapes), so older versions might not be able to read your files without compatibility mode. Thus, you might get a compatibility attention/option box, like the one in Figure 1-20.

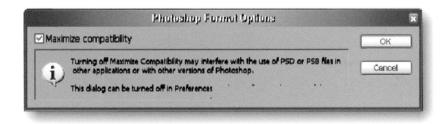

Figure 1-20: Consider backward-compatibility when saving to PSD.

• Select the Maximize Compatibility check box in this alert if you use Painter or Xara, or work with other users who haven't upgraded to Elements 4.

• If you never intend to share your PSD files with other Photoshop CS or Elements users, you don't need backward-compatibility — it just increases the saved file size a little.

RGB versus sRGB: No contest

The human eye is capable of understanding a great deal of color information; to simulate real-world scenes, red, green, and blue phosphors illuminate your monitor to faithfully reproduce these real-world colors. Adobe Systems created the Adobe RGB (1998) color profile to put your images into an RGB color space that looks natural and photographic in content. Elements calls this profile best for printing, but it's ideal for viewing pictures onscreen, too.

Unfortunately, there's a growing movement among manufacturers of digital cameras, scanners, and printers to use the *sRGB* (smallRGB or, more accurately, suckyRGB) color space. sRGB is a smaller color space than Adobe RGB. If you save to sRGB, you *clip* — discard — original image information unless your digital camera saves to sRGB, in which case the damage has already been done. In the figure here is a grid that represents all available light, including light that's not visible to humans, from 0 (no intensity) to 1.0 (full intensity). Within this space lies human vision, represented by the distorted, tongue-shaped spectrums of light — distorted because the human eye treats greens with disproportionate preference. Within the visible spectrum is Adobe RGB; it's smaller than our visible spectrum, but you usually don't notice this discrepancy on the monitor. And, inside RGB is sRGB; it's about 35 percent smaller than RGB color space. Note that every color within sRGB is also within RGB.

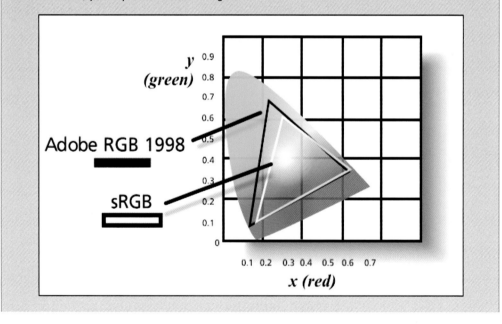

Why the push to a smaller inferior color space? First, don't trust the documentation that came with your camera; several manufacturers claim that their products save to sRGB to sound hip, but they don't. sRGB profiles make colors in images look juicy (in an unrealistic way), and manufacturers want to sell you on intense, brighter-than-bright output because the human eye is attracted to brilliant colors. The image therefore looks good (but unrealistic) when browsing your drive or the Web. In theory, if you save to sRGB and then print to an sRGB inkjet printer, you get better prints. My experience, however, is that sRGB output looks as subtle and accurate as a detergent box or a gum wrapper.

sRGB profiling can be done to PSD, TIF, JPEG, and SuperPNG file formats; sRGB is a structure within a file's information and not a file format.

Briefly, just say No to drugs, high-cholesterol foods, elective surgery, and sRGB.

TIFF options

The Tagged Image File Format standard is kept and improved upon by Adobe Systems. Like PSD, TIFF is RGB color although you can also save grayscale mode images to TIFF. *Selections* (areas in an image you mark as editable or, conversely, protected from editing) are covered in Book IV, Chapter 1; both PSD and TIFF can save selections to their file format.

A TIFF image created and saved in Elements can also save layers. Adobe included this feature to help out After Effects (a high-end Adobe movie editing program) users, but I recommend that you save images with layers to PSD format for two reasons:

+ Text and special effects layers lose their editability when saved in TIFF format.

+ Many applications can't import a TIFF image that contains layers.

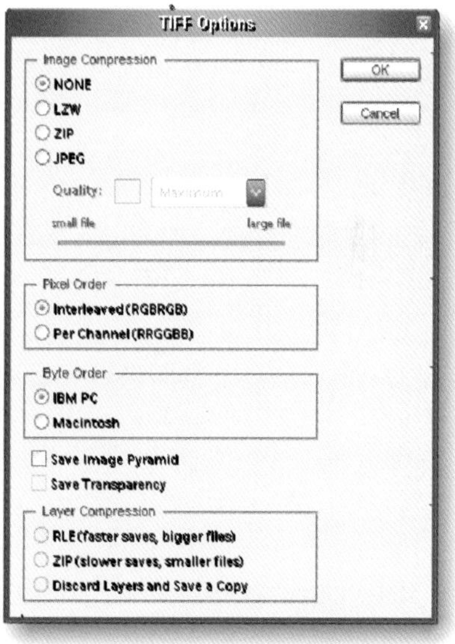

Figure 1-21 shows the TIFF Options dialog box, which appears when you choose to save a file as a TIFF. The important options deal mostly with *compression.* TIFF images can be written in a condensed way, to save hard drive space, without any loss of information. The images are then

Figure 1-21: TIFF is a close second to the robust PSD file format.

uncompressed when opened by Elements, without any need to call on a utility such as WinZip, and the compression is written *into* the image file.

The best file compression option depends on your hard drive space and to a minor extent your patience:

+ If your hard drive's nearly full, choose LZW or ZIP compression. Don't *ever* use JPEG compression — it's *lossy* compression, which I explain in the following JPEG section.

  Compressed files will save smaller but take a little longer to open.

+ If you have plenty of hard drive space to spare, use no compression. (This is the default.)

+ Leave the rest of the options at their default. However, don't select the Macintosh radio button if you're a Windows user, or any of the other options for layer saving (which I don't recommend).

Some applications that can import TIFF images cannot understand compression. Mostly, they're older versions of programs and programs that aren't design programs, such as word processors.

JPEG file format

JPEG is a compressed file format, which is why you see it all the time on the Web. However, JPEG has a critical fault for the serious photo editor: Its compression is *lossy* — some of the original image info is lost as you save.

Never save an original file to the JPEG format. If you need to save a file as a JPEG to post the image on the Web or to e-mail it, always save a copy of the image to preserve the original file.

The Elements command File➪Save for Web is better than choosing the usual File➪Save command and selecting to save the file as a JPEG. The Save For Web dialog box provides before and after preview windows to judge how much visual information is discarded with different Save settings.

As you can see in the upcoming Figure 1-23, you don't have to flatten a layered image to save a copy of it to JPEG. Just follow these steps:

1. Choose File➪Save for Web and then choose JPEG Medium from the Presets drop-down list.

2. **If the preview looks pixellated (see Figure 1-22), click the right-arrow button to the right of the Quality field and drag the slider that pops up to the right until the preview looks acceptable.**

3. **The other settings for JPEG export are shown in this list:**

   - Select the Progressive check box if you want to speed up the display of a JPEG while it's downloading to someone's Web browser. A progressive JPEG begins assembling itself as it downloads in a sort of crude-to-refined animated representation until the entire image has been downloaded.

Figure 1-22: JPEG figures look grungy up close.

   - Select the ICC Profile check box.

     This action preserves the color space. (See the preceding sidebar, "RGB versus sRGB: No contest.")

At the bottom of the After preview panel in the Save For Web dialog box, (see Figure 1-23) you can see the saved file size. This amount is measured in kilobytes, and in my experience it's an approximation. In Windows, open the drive window where the JPEG has been written and check the actual file size afterward; before you upload the file, I suggest that you do the following to ensure that Elements is writing a JPEG you want and need:

   - Keep e-mail attachments to less than 50K, as a courtesy to your friends who have dial-up connections and because many forums have a 100K file limit.

   - If your image is just too darned large, scale it by using the New Size field.

4. **After you save the JPEG, choose Edit⇨Revert.**

   Otherwise, you get a Save Changes dialog box even though you didn't change the original image.

Your digital camera probably saves to JPEG but only at about a 10:1 ratio, so the damage isn't too bad. However, JPEG quality deteriorates to a visible extent *with every subsequent save.* Save to PSD as a routine — PSD includes some lossless compression, so you're not squandering bytes.

Figure 1-23: Use the Save for Web command to save and preview JPEG exports.

The xnview freeware utility for Windows, Macintosh, and Linux (from www. xnview.com) can rotate JPEG images without any loss of image quality. If you rotate your camera to take a picture in portrait orientation, you can "unrotate" the image before editing it in Elements.

PNG file format

The Portable Network Graphics file format is becoming the hands-down choice for compressed, high-quality images. PNG compression is just a little larger than the same files as a JPEG, but PNG allows transparency and doesn't reduce image quality *(lossless compression).*

PNG is terrific for archiving purposes.

The color mode is RGB. Just about all the images for this book (and most of the images on my hard drive) were saved to PNG.

PNGs can include *transparency,* areas within the image that don't show up onscreen (but only one layer). If you have an image with one layer — a *flat* image — follow these steps to write the image to the PNG file format:

1. **Choose File⇨Save As.**

   Choose PNG from the Format drop-down list.

2. **Clear the As a Copy check box (as shown in Figure 1-24).**

   Elements saves the file with image transparency, if your image *has* transparency (a single-layer file where you can see the checkered background). Name the file and then click Save.

3. **The PNG Options dialog box appears. Don't mark the Interlaced radio button unless you're saving for a Web page and you know that your audience has slow Internet connections.**

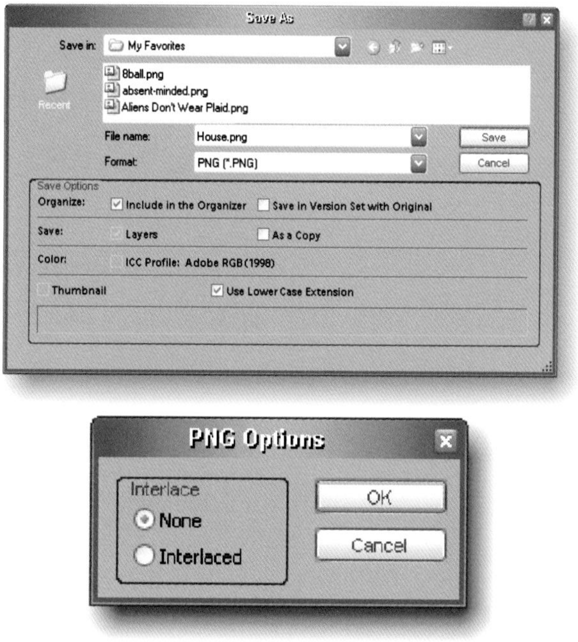

Figure 1-24: PNG is becoming the preferred file format for imaging professionals.

TIP

PNG is the file format for icons in Windows Vista. With Elements, you can create your own desktop and shortcut icons.

PNG: Forever free and the archiver's friend

PNG was designed to quell some squabbles over JPEG and GIF (whose file format custodians occasionally send murmurs of collecting royalties per image to users of those formats). PNG will always be royalty-free.

GIF file format

The GIF file format is on the low rung of photographic-quality imaging.

GIF's color capacity is a maximum of 256 unique colors. In comparison, photographs have a capacity of 16.7 million colors. Mathematically (and often visually), GIF images lose something in the translation.

You can get away with a GIF copy of your work (if the dimensions of the file are small — 50K or around 200 x 200 pixels) if you use

✦ **Selective color-ordering:** This is the default for Elements.

✦ **Diffusion dithering:** Scattering colors to make the picture look as though there are more colors.

GIF has a couple of advantages:

✦ The saved GIF file size is often smaller than a JPEG equivalent.

✦ GIFs are the only "official" animation format for the Web.

MPEGs — actual sound-capable movies, compressed according to the standards of the Motion Picture Experts Group — are usually way too large, and Flash files are usually *vector* compositions (so Flash files cannot be created using Elements).

Adobe acquired Macromedia in fall 2005, thus acquiring Flash technology. Stay tuned: Elements 5 might include Flash tools.

It's best to save a file as a GIF by choosing File⇨Save for Web. In Figure 1-25, you can see that this house image looks okay in the preview window — but it's not a photo, and therefore contains few unique colors.

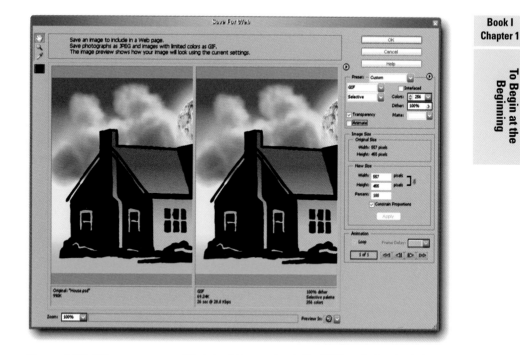

Figure 1-25: GIF images are small but should be used only if a JPEG equivalent looks bad.

Determining how many colors are in an image is sometimes difficult; it's therefore more difficult to determine in advance how many colors will be preserved when you save a copy to GIF, which Elements calls *Indexed color mode,* not RGB. If you question how well a particular image will turn out as a GIF copy, choose File⇨Duplicate so that you're not messing with your original image. Then choose Image⇨Mode⇨Indexed Color and accept the defaults. Choose Image⇨Mode⇨Color Table and check out the palette of colors used to represent the original photo. If the resulting image looks okay and the colors are faithful to the original, just choose File⇨Save and save to GIF format without using the Save for Web command. If the colors in the color table look wrong, try a different dithering option with your original image: Perceptual, Adaptive, and Selective are all available in the Save for Web dialog box.

You can safely and successfully export most images to GIF format by choosing File⇨Save for Web without changing the image's mode and looking at its color table.

Chapter 2: Checking Out the Elements Workspaces

*U*nderstanding how to use something before using it is important — I'm reminded of my painful first experience with a radial saw. The Elements Editor, the main module that I cover in this book, is highly customizable, so you can set your own work style to work more quickly in it. At the same time that Elements needs your input — like scratch disk locations and memory allocation to operate efficiently — it needs some system info so that it can run better.

Adobe Systems has no idea who you are, so it includes a massive Preferences list by which you can turn Photoshop Elements into Mike's Elements or Gwen's Elements, for example. A customized work environment is as pleasant as getting some plants and hanging your first picture in your new home. I also cover the Elements menus in this chapter — the menu has important features that you can't access by any other means. Because you have so many choices, I extend my options coverage to Chapter 3.

To begin the tour, launch Elements, choosing the Editor from the welcome screen. (Click the Edit and Enhance Photos icon there. If this is foreign soil to you, see Chapter 1 of this mini-book.) You can find all sample files that I use in this chapter from www.dummies.com/go/PhotoshopElementsAIOFD1e.

What Looks Good on the Elements Menu?

Whenever you buy and install any application, cruising the menus is a wise first move.

Elements has a lot of menu options, with quite a few menu commands. Accessing a command shouldn't require that you mouse clear up to the menu all the time; it's a distraction, and I offer shortcuts for menu commands throughout this chapter.

The File menu

Begin at the beginning: the File menu (see Figure 2-1).

New	▶
Create	▶
Open...	Ctrl+O
Open As...	Alt+Ctrl+O
Open Recently Edited File	▶
Duplicate...	
Close	Ctrl+W
Close All	Alt+Ctrl+W
Save	Ctrl+S
Save As...	Shift+Ctrl+S
Save for Web...	Alt+Shift+Ctrl+S
Attach to Email...	
File Info...	
Place...	
Organize Open Files...	
Process Multiple Files...	
Import	▶
Export	▶
Automation Tools	▶
Page Setup...	Shift+Ctrl+P
Print...	Ctrl+P
Print Multiple Photos...	Alt+Ctrl+P
Order Prints...	
Exit	Ctrl+Q

Figure 2-1: The File menu.

The following sections list common Windows commands and specific Elements commands for the File menu.

The standard Windows commands

The File menu contains mostly common Windows items:

✦ **New, Ctrl+N:** Choose File⇨New to create a new file. (Go figure.) Or, even simpler, Ctrl+double-click the workspace.

Here are the items you need to set after choosing File⇨New:

- **Size:** The New dialog box (see the upcoming Figure 2-2) offers different sizes of images; by default, if anything is on the Windows Clipboard — even text — Elements offers a new file based on the Clipboard contents.

  I offer image dimensions throughout this book for different projects. If you're starting a new image, select a size from the Preset drop-down list (see Figure 2-2).

- **Color Mode:** I get into image Color Mode later in this chapter; for now, you'll be happiest with RGB Color.

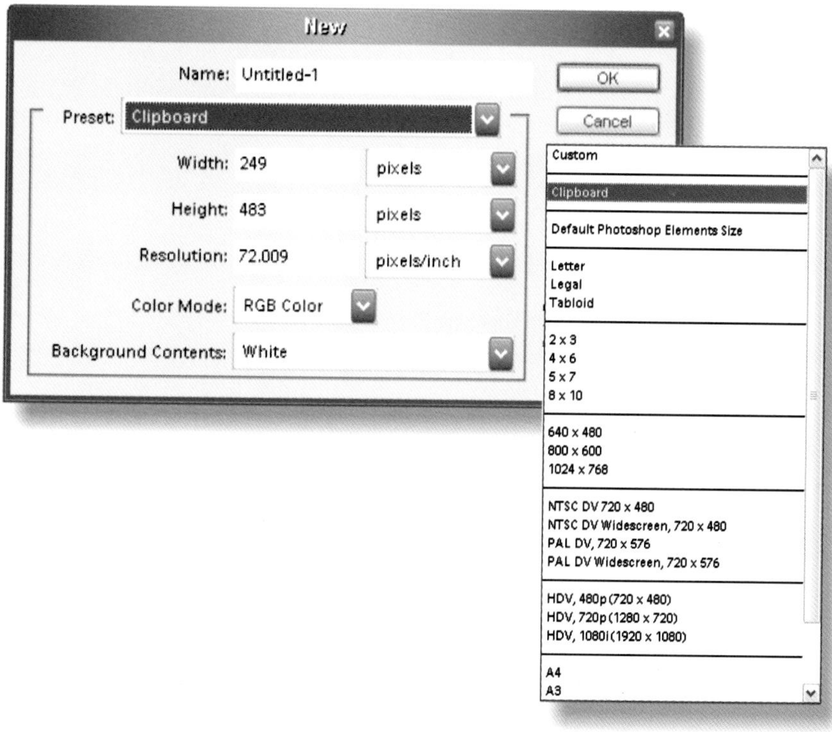

Figure 2-2: Select a size from the Preset drop-down list.

- **Background Contents:** As far as the Background Contents goes, Elements offers

  - *White:* This is a good place to start painting.

  - *Background Color:* This is the color of the background swatch on the Toolbox.

  - *Transparent:* A *transparent* background is actually a layer that contains no pixels, not even white ones. The whole concept of image transparency deserves its own section — I refer you to Book V, Chapter 1, which covers image layers.

✦ **Open, Ctrl+O:** Choose File⇨Open to access this command.

Double-clicking the workspace to bring up the Open dialog box is easier. You also see New, Open, and Save icons below the main menu, but, again, I'm not a big fan of needlessly running up miles on my mouse.

✦ **Open As:** Choose File⇨Open As to open a file that a user didn't label with a file extension. You have to guess the file type. This happens because Macintosh users sometimes don't add file extensions; the Mac OS doesn't need them.

Your best bet is to try PSD first; then try TIFF if PSD doesn't work.

✦ **Open Recently Edited File:** Choose File⇨Open Recently Edited File to see a list of the files you've recently worked in.

You don't have to edit a file to find this command on the list — it appears if you've opened a file in Elements. You can customize the Recently Edited list through General Preferences (see Figure 2-3); I get to this topic later in this chapter.

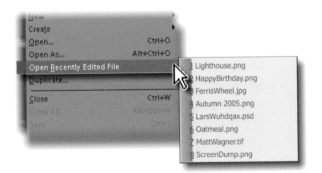

Figure 2-3: Customizing the Recently Edited list.

✦ **Duplicate:** Choose File⇨Duplicate to create an unsaved copy of your work at the exact point in time when you call the command.

The Duplicate command comes in handy when you're uncertain of your editing work: Duplicate the image (in the Duplicate Image dialog box, give the duplicate an easy name to remember — Elements uses the original's filename and tacks the word *copy* at the end), click the title bar of the original, and then choose Edit⇨Revert. You then have a version of the original, plus all your edits.

+ **Close, Ctrl+W:** Choose File⇨Close to close a file.

The usual Windows command Ctrl+F4 works in Elements, too.

+ **Close All:** Choose File⇨Close All to close all open files in Elements.

+ **Save/Save As:** Choose File⇨Save or File⇨Save As to save the changes you made to an image. Ctrl+S is the Windows shortcut for saving files, and Elements accepts this shortcut.

Use the Save As command when you want an edited copy of your work.

+ **Save for Web:** Choose File⇨Save for Web to save an image as a GIF (and animated GIF), JPEG, or PNG and preserve the original file.

This is a mostly unneeded command. Regular unanimated GIFs, JPEGs, and PNGs can be saved by pressing Ctrl+S without using Save for Web. To use the Save for Web command, you must either

  • Save a new image.

  • Choose Edit⇨Revert for an existing image (or you get an unwanted dialog box even though you haven't changed the image).

+ **Attach to Email:** Choose File⇨Attach to Email to create an e-mail message with the open file as an attachment.

This command is unnecessary; you can do this task in your mail browser.

+ **Page Setup:** Choose File⇨Page Setup to specify page dimensions for printing, the printer you want to use, and (by digging into the child dialog boxes until you reach the Advanced button) the number of dots per inch (dpi) you want to print. You've probably seen the dialog box, called from Windows, in other applications, such as Word.

This command is common in other Windows-compliant programs.

+ **Print:** Choose File⇨Print (or press Ctrl+P, a standard Windows command) to print your images.

Here are some other Print options:

  • *Print Multiple Copies:* This command moves you to the Organizer module, which I explain in Book I, Chapter 1.

  • *Order Prints:* This command resulted from a deal that Adobe made with Kodak to allow you to order prints online. It has nothing to do with the Elements Editor.

TIP

IPTC spells safety

Elements uses the IPTC standard to identify and protect your work, even if you're not a Jimmy Olsen. The IPTC (International Press Tele-communications Council) was established in 1965 by a group of news organizations, including Associated Press and the now-defunct United Press International, to safeguard telecommunications.

The commands in the preceding list are common commands, and you have likely seen and used many of them in other programs.

The File/File Info command

The File Info command (choose File⇨File Info) enables you to view and edit detailed information about an image.

Using this command is how you can save information (such as your name and address) and copyright your work for posting on the Web.

To embed (invisible) text info into an image, get out any image (a JPEG, for example), and follow these steps:

1. **With your image open, choose File⇨File Info.**

   You don't have to fill in every field; start with Description.

2. **Enter the name of the picture.**

   It doesn't have to be a file name, and an extension isn't needed.

3. **Type your name in the Author field.**

4. **The Caption field is a good place to enter the location and year of your creation as well as any notes to yourself.**

   If you post this image to the Internet, anyone who has Elements or an image organizer that displays IPTC info can read your caption.

5. **Enter copyright data.**

   - **Copyright Status:** If the image legally belongs to you, fill in the Copyright Status field. Elements, Photoshop, and many other programs display a copyright symbol on the left side of an image's title bar when you choose this setting.

   - **Holder and Date:** Enter the name of the copyright holder and date.

   - **Copyright Notice:** If you reserve all rights (or don't want to allow others to use the image), fill in this field.

6. In the IPTC Contact field, type your e-mail address; see Figure 2-4.

Figure 2-4: Enter copyright info here.

This step not only discourages the possible theft of your picture if it's posted to the Web, but also makes it easy for friends and customers to contact you.

The Camera Data fields are automatically filled out by your digital camera when you dump your camera's reader card to your hard drive. The IPTC fields don't need to be completed; photojournalists add data there when they transmit photos to newspapers, and some of the data you enter in the Description fields is automatically copied there. To the best of my knowledge, spambots can't read IPTC data in a posted image. In Figure 2-5, you can see this fairly effortless process.

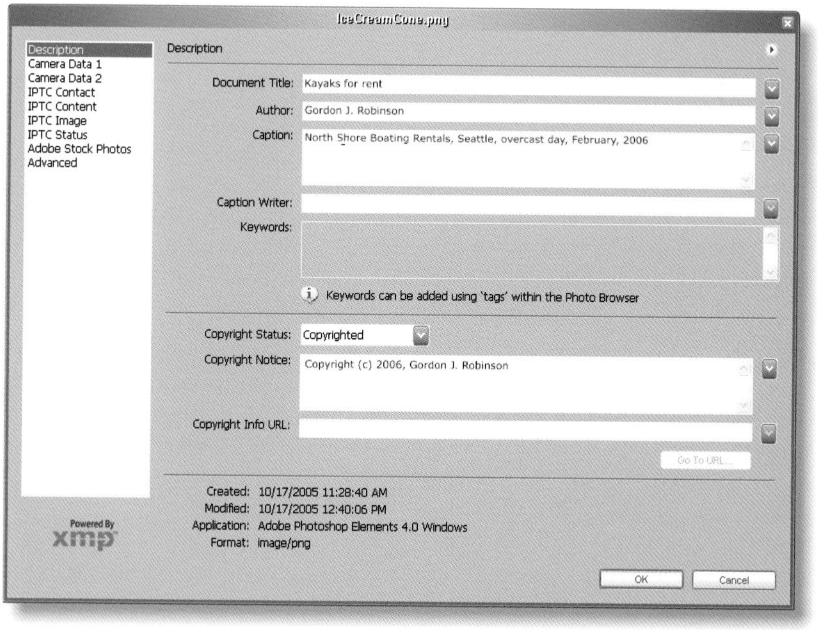

Figure 2-5: Use File Info to add text data about an image and your e-mail contact.

Elements remembers fields when you embed text. To save typing time, click the flyout arrow next to a field and then click the entry.

7. **Click OK and save the file.**

In Figure 2-6, you can see the result I got by adding File Info. Note the little copyright symbol on the title bar of my image. For your most valuable work, some protection is better than none, so use File Info for personal reference and copyright announcements.

Figure 2-6: Copyrighting your images announces your intentions to the Internet community.

If you post to the Web, be prepared to give away your work. Others can download and "borrow" (cough, *steal*) your work even though you copyrighted it. Other users of Photoshop or Elements can change your data. Even IPTC members (you're not a member just because you use its file data feature) can have their data removed, but it's not worth the effort for ethical people.

A good countermeasure is to post only very small images, smaller than 300 x 300 pixels — too small for an art thief to repurpose or print.

The File/Place command

The Place command (choose File⇨Place) is a method for adding images on layers to an open image, which saves Clipboard resources. (As a rule, don't use the traditional copy and paste method but instead use the Elements internal copying features I describe throughout the book.)

Although most of the files you work with in Elements are bitmaps, you can use the Place command to add vector graphics to your image. The two graphics formats work differently:

✦ **Bitmap graphics:** Also called *raster graphics* by nerds, *bitmap* graphics are literally a map of bits of image information.

The building block of a bitmap is the pixel. A *pixel* is a unit, a placeholder filled with color; it's not a unit of measurement like miles or calories or anything. Pixels are ordered in an imaginary grid (the *map* part of the term bitmap). The *resolution* of an image of a bitmap image is expressed as how many *pixels per inch* (or centimeters) the image measures. A bitmap image contains a finite number of pixels no matter how you measure it, and this is why bitmaps are called *resolution-dependent.*

An image editor (such as Elements) has a couple of limitations when you're making a bitmap image larger or smaller:

- It cannot make a bitmap smaller without discarding pixels.

- It cannot increase an image's dimensions without guessing what color the additional pixels need to be — and the result looks awful.

✦ **Vector graphics:** *Vector* graphics use math equations to describe shapes. Typical file extensions for vector graphics are PS, AI, and EPS. You might also see CDR, XAR, and others, but Elements imports only AI, PS, and EPS file formats.

By using math, a vector graphic can be scaled without losing design quality. For example, if you want a design twice the size you drew it, the application adds a *times two* to the saved file's math, which is simpler than it might sound.

Vector graphics aren't photographed but instead are created and designed using the program's drawing tools; Illustrator and Xara are vector drawing programs. Clip art is usually saved as vectors to Illustrator (`*.ai`) format. However, you can't see a vector math equation, so the application draws to your screen (your screen displays one big bitmap, refreshed from moment to moment) — and Elements can place a vector file, rendering it to bitmap format so it truly becomes part of your compositions.

To place a vector design in an image, open any bitmap image (I used my file `DriveIn.png`), and then follow these steps:

1. **Choose File⇨Place and browse for a vector graphic file.**

   If you don't have a vector graphic handy, you can download my `Refreshments.ai` file to your hard drive from www.dummies.com/ go/PhotoshopElementsAIOFD1e.

2. **Click in the image window to place the vector graphic.**

   The vector graphic is added on a new layer to the image.

   Although you probably haven't touched the Move tool (on the Toolbox; see Book I, Chapter 3), this tool is active, and the placed graphic is in Free Transform mode, which enables you to rotate, resize, and generally distort a selected image area. I explain this topic in more detail in later chapters.

3. **Click the link proportions icon (the little chain link image between the width and height fields, on the Options bar).**

   This step keeps the graphic's proportions in scale as you decrease or increase its size. By default, Elements fills the image window with a placed vector graphic.

4. **To scale the graphic:**

   a. *Drag one of the corner Free Transform bounding box handles toward the center of the graphic.*

   b. *Reposition the graphic by dragging anywhere inside the "x"-ed box.*

5. **Press Enter (or click the check icon on the Options bar) to finalize the import (the placed vector graphic).**

See the result in Figure 2-7.

Figure 2-7: A placed vector graphic becomes a bitmap after you finalize its placement.

The File/Import command

The Import command (choose File⇨Import) is reserved for

+ Plug-ins that use this command
+ Capturing a frame of a video from MPEG or AVI movie files

Using Frame from Video is a free way to extract movie stills: Movie-capture utilities can cost serious bucks. Unlike capturing screenshots of other programs, you can't press the Print Screen key to capture a frame of an MPEG or AVI file because they're played on a reserved video layer onscreen.

To capture a frame from an MPEG or AVI movie, follow these steps:

1. **Choose File⇨Import.**

2. **In the Import dialog box that appears, click the Browse button to find and then open the movie.**

   The dialog box for this import command opens.

3. **To browse through the film frames and capture one or more frames:**

a. *Use the VCR-like controls in the dialog box for coarse selection.*

b. *Use your keyboard's left- and right-arrow keys to home in on a specific frame.*

4. Click the Grab Frame button.

You can repeat Step 4 to extract multiple stills from a movie. The extracted frames appear in the workspace, named and numbered in sequence. Figure 2-8 shows how to capture a single movie frame.

The stills have no file format. Although you can edit them, you must save them as you do with any of your work.

Figure 2-8: Capture movie stills for import.

Here are two notes on extracting video frames:

✦ Make sure you have permission to copy a film frame. Personal use is okay if you want to make desktop wallpaper. However, commercial movies are protected by copyrights, so you can't capture, edit, and then post images — say, of Darth Vader — to the Web.

✦ MPEG images are small resolution, typically only 350 x 240 pixels, which is suitable for display on low-resolution TVs. Thus, they're typically too tiny to edit and save as anything that looks good onscreen — and forget about printing the captures.

The Edit menu

The Edit menu is made up of a combination of standard Windows commands, plus some valuable image editing items (see Figure 2-9).

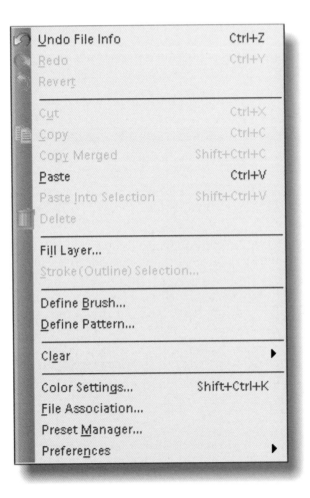

Figure 2-9: The Edit menu.

The standard Windows commands

The following list describes the basic commands on the Edit menu:

✦ **Copy, Ctrl+C:** Choose Edit➪Copy to copy a selection to the Clipboard.

✦ **Cut, Ctrl+X:** Choose Edit➪Cut to cut the contents of a selection in an image and put it on the Clipboard. Pressing Backspace or Delete cuts a selection's contents but doesn't put it on the Clipboard. Depending on whether you're cutting from a plain image or a layered image, cutting produces different results:

- *When you use the Cut command on a selection on the Background layer,* the selected area is replaced with the current background color on the Toolbox.

- *When you use the Cut command on a selection on a layer in a composition,* the selection area becomes transparent (no color is substituted).

✦ **Copy Merged:** Choose Edit➪Copy Merged to copy a selection area composed of image pixels on every layer in an image window — except for layers that are hidden from view. (You can tell which layers are hidden because their eye icon is turned off on the Layers palette.)

Copy Merged is a handy feature when you want to paste a selection into applications that can't handle image transparency, such as Word and the Windows Calculator.

✦ **Revert:** Choose Edit➪Revert to reject all edits made to an image since it was last saved.

✦ **Undo (Ctrl+Z)/Redo (Ctrl+Y):** Choose Edit➪Undo and Edit➪Redo to step backward and forward, respectively, in your image editing.

Carefully check the workspace for changes you've made to brush sizes, the current image editing layer, and other custom settings after you press Ctrl+Z. Undo applies to both paint strokes layer-blending modes and the general environment you defined in Elements.

Using the Undo History palette is much quicker if you need to undo more than a few edits. It's covered in the later section, "The Window menu."

✦ **Paste Into Selection:** Choose Edit➪Paste Into Selection to paste from the Clipboard without adding a layer to your composition.

By default, pasted items are automatically added to a new image layer.

✦ **Fill Selection:** Choose Edit➪Fill Selection to fill a selected area with a solid color or with a pattern. (To fill with foreground color from the Toolbox press Alt+Backspace.)

This command isn't as useful as manually filling a selection although it merits an explanation because you can use it to begin filling images without reading Book I, Chapter 3. A selection can exist on a layer, even an empty layer; it's an entity independent of the actual image data. When you choose to fill a selection, you have the option of filling with a color or a pattern. If you choose Pattern, you can select one from Elements' preset patterns or one you saved beforehand (see Figure 2-10). In any event, you have additional options for the amount of opacity of the fill as well as which blending mode to use. (Both are explained in Book V, Chapter 3.)

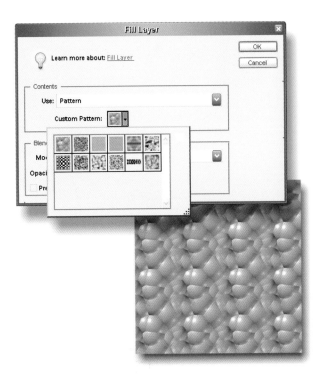

Figure 2-10: Choosing a pattern.

✦ **Stroke Selection:** Choose Edit➪Stroke Selection to make a border out of a selection. Use the Stroke Selection command to add a stroke on a new layer, keeping the original layer intact.

In Figure 2-11, I created a crescent moon selection and then applied a stroke that's 6 pixels wide.

✦ **Define Brush and Define Fill:** The Edit commands sample a selection's contents and turn them into brush tips and pattern fills:

- Choose Edit➪Define Brush to build your own paintbrush tips from bitmap images.

   See Book I, Chapter 3 for more about the Define Brush command.

- Choose Edit➪Define Fill to create your own fills from bitmaps.

   The Define Fill command is covered in Book VI, Chapter 3.

✦ **Clear:** Choose Edit➪Clear to either

- *Purge the Clipboard,* which deletes the Clipboard contents and thus restores free system RAM.

- *Purge the edits in the Undo History palette,* which frees some of the system RAM that Elements is using.

WARNING!

If Elements is performing sluggishly, purge the Undo History palette and Clipboard with this command but *only after you paste the Clipboard contents you need.*

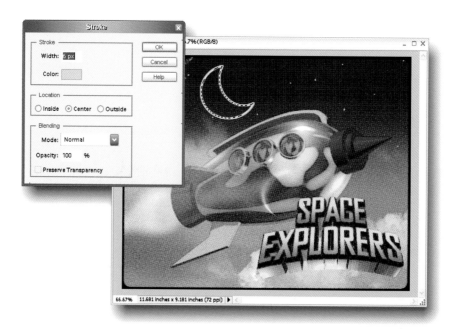

Figure 2-11: Stroking a selection creates an outline design.

EPS file extensions

Encapsulated PostScript (EPS) is written in two different ways and should have two different file extensions because there's one EPS flavor that Elements doesn't work with. EPS files containing vector information are the ones Elements can place. They're a generic version of Adobe Illustrator AI files, but a legal issue is involved with tagging Illustrator files with the EPS extension if Illustrator didn't create the file. Then there's the issue of Placeable EPS files: These files contain printer information (no printer vector instructions are included), and this type of file doesn't open in most applications but is instead placed on a document page in a program, such as InDesign as printer instructions. Unfortunately, you have no way to tell the difference between the two except by choosing File➪Place; if you get an error dialog box, it's the wrong kind of EPS file.

The Edit/Color settings

The Color Settings dialog box (choose Edit⇨Color Settings) is a critical area of Elements: It defines how image color space is handled and preserved. Your options are

✦ **No Color Management:** This option is an unwise choice because Windows XP has no native color management utilities (also called *color profiling*).

✦ **Always Optimize Colors for Computer Screens:** Select this radio button to profile and save images to the sRGB (small RGB) color space.

The term *color space* has to do with the quality of colors saved in your images. Many cameras, scanners, and inkjet printers use sRGB for intense, Kodachrome-ish image colors, but this doesn't mean that you need to use sRGB. This color space is around 20 percent smaller than actual RGB (Adobe RGB). If you choose this option, many subtle colors in photographs taken and saved to actual RGB will be *clipped* (eliminated).

✦ **Always Optimize for Printing:** My advice is to be a pro with Elements:

• Select the Always Optimize for Printing radio button to save your work in the largest color space Elements offers (see Figure 2-12). Always Optimize for Printing doesn't work just for prints; it also preserves original image colors for screen display.

• Choose Adobe RGB (1998) as your color profile for new and saved images.

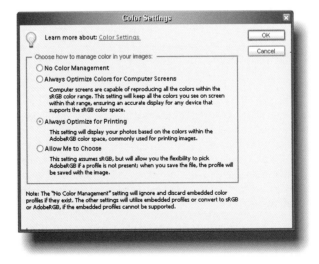

Figure 2-12: Color Settings define the color space of your new and saved images.

✦ **Allow Me to Choose:** The last option in the Color Settings dialog box enables you to decide on a case-by-case basis what color space you want to use.

This is a distraction you don't need as you work.

The File Association command and the Preset Manager

The File Association command on the Edit menu enables you to define what program opens a certain type of bitmap image when you double-click an icon on the desktop or in Windows Explorer. I suggest that you assign BMP, JPG, GIF, and PNG to Windows Picture and Fax Viewer by choosing Tools⇨Folder Options⇨File Types, accessed through a drive window instead of associating it with Elements because it loads a lot quicker than Elements does, particularly when you want only to preview a file. When you want to open these files in Elements for editing, you can either

✦ Open Elements and choose File⇨Open.

or

✦ Drag the file icon into the Elements workspace.

The Preset Manager command on the Edit menu can be used for determining which palette is loaded for brushes and other tools. Not a key Elements feature, it's unnecessarily complicated for novices.

Making your Preferences clear

Preferences are so important that you have a keyboard shortcut — Ctrl+K — to get you to the Preferences dialog box to set such vital user options such as memory management and cursor display.

Elements stuffs tons of options into the Preferences dialog box — so many options that Adobe can't display all the tabs that would be needed to group these options. So you move forward and backward through multiple, grouped Preferences menus:

✦ Select the type of preferences that you want to see by choosing an option from the drop-down list at the top of the Preferences dialog box. The Preferences dialog box updates to show you just the options for that selection.

✦ Click the Next and Prev buttons — like using a standard wizard — to move through the different sets of options in the Preferences dialog box.

General Preferences

Select General from the top drop-down list to see the General Preferences options. This is where you make the least specific but still important choices; see Figure 2-13.

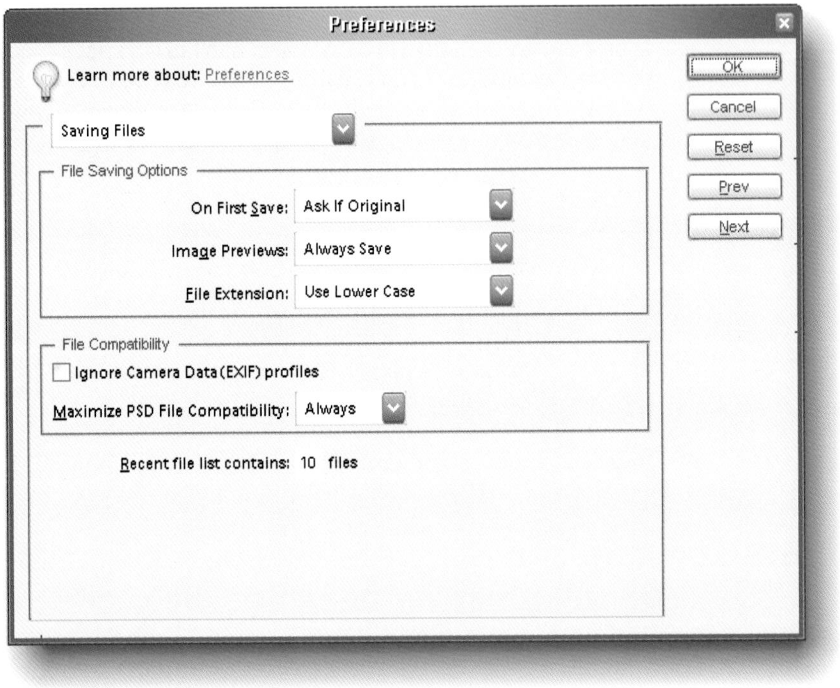

Preferences	✕

Learn more about: Preferences

OK
Cancel
Reset
Prev
Next

Saving Files ▾

File Saving Options

On First Save: Ask If Original ▾

Image Previews: Always Save ▾

File Extension: Use Lower Case ▾

File Compatibility

☐ Ignore Camera Data (EXIF) profiles

Maximize PSD File Compatibility: Always ▾

Recent file list contains: 10 files

Figure 2-13: The General Preferences options apply to the most common tasks in Elements.

✦ **Color Picker:** The Color Picker drop-down list enables you to select the Color Picker that's used when you click the foreground or background swatches on the Toolbox.

Choosing Adobe from the Color Picker drop-down list enables you to choose colors from a Hue, Saturation, Brightness model, or straight RGB; it also tells you what the HTML (Web) color equivalent is. These benefits are not offered when you select the Windows option from the Color Picker drop-down list.

✦ **Step Back/Fwd:** Leave this drop-down list at the default choice (Ctrl+Z/ Ctrl+Y); you'd be hard-pressed to find an easier-to-remember set of keyboard shortcuts for undoing and redoing editing moves.

✦ **History States:** The History States text box enables you to change how many steps in editing you can undo by using the Undo History palette if you make a mistake. By default, you get 50 undos.

You might be tempted to enter a higher number in the History States number box so you can go back even farther in the Undo History palette. However, each step that's stored in the Undo History palette requires system resources and temporary hard drive space. Unless your system is stocked to the gills with RAM and hard drive space, you might want to reduce the number in the History States text box to about 20. You probably know when you've made an editing error no more than five steps ago.

✦ **Export Clipboard:** Make sure that this check box is selected.

If you clear the Export Clipboard check box, other applications can't paste from Elements.

✦ **Show Tool Tips:** By default, little titles appear next to a tool when you hover your cursor over it.

There's no harm in leaving this check box selected. However, if you find Tool Tips distracting (see an example in the figure here), clear the Show Tool Tips check box.

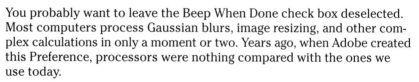

✦ **Zoom Resizes Windows:** Leave this check box selected. It's a pain to have to manually expand a window after you zoom in. This option also appears on the Options bar when the Zoom tool is chosen.

✦ **Beep When Done:** Selecting this check box causes Elements to beep to alert you that a process has finished.

You probably want to leave the Beep When Done check box deselected. Most computers process Gaussian blurs, image resizing, and other complex calculations in only a moment or two. Years ago, when Adobe created this Preference, processors were nothing compared with the ones we use today.

✦ **Select Move Tool After Committing Text:** Elements presumes that after you create text, you'll want to move it, so the program toggles to the Move tool when this check box is selected.

✦ **Save Palette Locations:** When this check box is selected, Elements remembers where you left a palette in the workspace the last time you closed the program.

Select this check box to make your editing work easier.

✦ **Use Shift Key for Tool Switch:** You can toggle between tools in a tool group by pressing Shift when you have this check box selected.

Just click the tool you want from the Options bar. It's easier.

✦ **Center Document Windows:** When this check box is selected, Elements places the window containing a newly opened file in the center of the screen.

✦ **Relaxed Text Selection:** This preference enables you to select text by using the Move tool. Click+drag anywhere in the image window.

This option is unnecessary, so leave it deselected.

✦ **Photo Bin Auto-Hide:** Select this check box to hide thumbnails of all the files open in the workspace.

✦ **Zoom with Scroll Wheel:** If you have a mouse with a wheel between left and right buttons, check this item. Then use the mouse wheel to zoom in and out of a photo when any tool is selected. Neat!

Saving Files Preferences

Click the Next button or choose Saving Files from the top drop-down list in the Preferences dialog box (refer to Figure 2-13) to see the options for saving files. The following list describes your file-saving options:

✦ **On First Save:** Elements can stop you from accidentally overwriting a precious original file if you choose Always Ask from the drop-down list.

✦ **Image Previews:** Choosing Always Save from this drop-down list adds only about 5K to a saved file, so do it.

With a preview, you can view a file in the Open dialog box without actually opening it. Few people want to accidentally load an 18MB file that has an obscure name just to see what it is.

✦ **File Extension:** I suggest that you choose Use Lower Case from this drop-down list because reading lowercase letters is easier on the eyes than uppercase.

✦ **Ignore Camera Data (EXIF) Profiles:** Deselect this check box; you want camera data profiles in your images because digital cameras often write valuable color information to the header of an image file.

This information can be accessed by choosing File➪File Info.

✦ **Maximize PSD File Compatibility:** Choosing Always from this drop-down list *plumps up* — increases — a saved PSD file, but other programs such as Painter might not read the PSD file.

If you use Elements only for image editing, either

- Turn compatibility off by choosing Never from the drop-down list.

  or

- Choose Ask to see a dialog box when you save an image that asks you to decide whether you want to maximize compatibility.

✦ **Recent File List Contains *x* Files:** Try entering **10** in this number box. It's nice to be able to see that many files when you choose File➪Open Recently Edited File. The number you enter here doesn't affect system memory or application speed, so enter any number up to, and including, 30.

Display & Cursors Preferences

Click the Next button or choose Display & Cursors from the top drop-down list in the Preferences dialog box to see the options for display settings and cursors. The following list describes the Display & Cursors options:

✦ **Use Pixel Doubling:** Selecting this check box provides a slightly more accurate view of a photo when you zoom in and out.

It's not worth the system resources it requires.

✦ **Painting Cursors:** The Brush, Clone, and other Toolbox tools you use to apply color pixels to an image can appear onscreen using different cursors. I recommend that you select these preferences:

- Normal Brush Tip radio button

  When the Full Size Brush Tip check box is selected, Elements displays the extent of the brush size (and with soft tips, the cursor display acts sluggishly).

- Show Crosshair in Brush Tip check box

  The crosshair always shows you the dead center of your brush for accuracy. You don't really need to watch the tool icon as you paint.

✦ **Other Cursors:** Select the Standard option button; the standard cursor display suits most jobs.

If you need pinpoint accuracy while you're editing (making a selection with the Lasso tool, for example), press the Caps Lock key to switch the tool to Precise cursor display.

Transparency Preferences

An image area that contains no pixels is displayed as a faint checkerboard pattern. If you're editing an image of a checkerboard pattern, though, you might want to change the size and color of the default checkerboard pattern that Elements uses to display transparency. Also, if you're editing a grayscale image, the edges of the opaque areas on a layer are much easier to see if you choose an obnoxious green or red checkerboard pattern for transparency (see Figure 2-14).

Figure 2-14: Comparing transparency effects.

To change the transparency options, open the Preferences dialog box (if it isn't already open) and select Transparency in the top drop-down list. See Figure 2-15.

Use the Grid Size drop-down list to select how large or small Elements should make the checkerboard pattern. The Grid Colors drop-down list enables you to choose how light or dark you want the checkerboard pattern. Finally, you can click the white and gray squares below the drop-down lists to choose different colors for the checkerboard pattern.

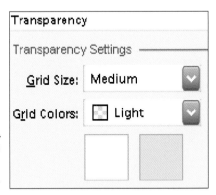

Figure 2-15: Set the look of Elements cursors and image transparency onscreen.

Units & Rulers Preferences

Click the Next button or choose Units & Rulers from the top drop-down list in the Preferences dialog box to see the options for rulers, guidelines, and units of measurement (see Figure 2-16).

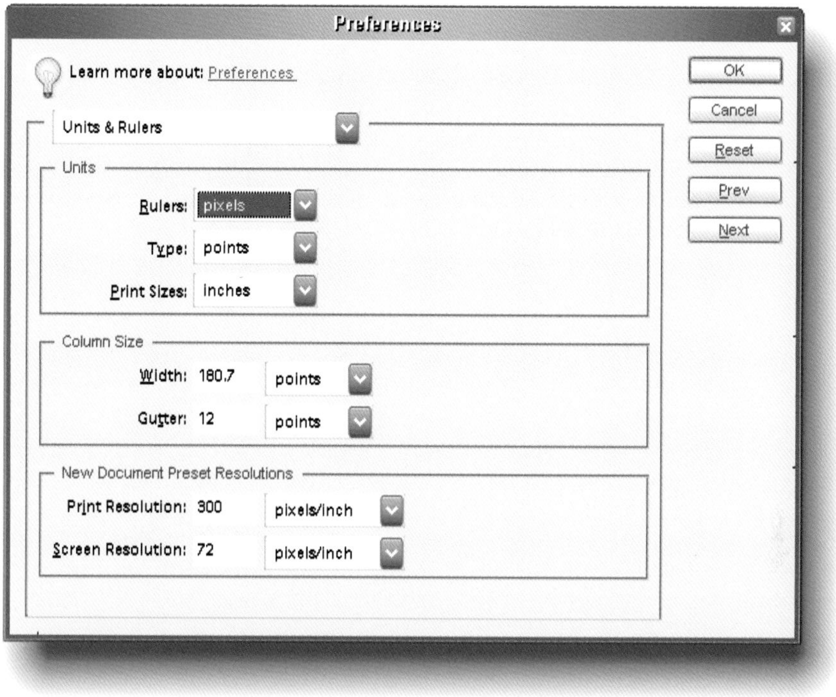

Preferences

Learn more about: Preferences

OK

Cancel

Reset

Prev

Next

Units & Rulers

Units

Rulers: pixels

Type: points

Print Sizes: inches

Column Size

Width: 180.7   points

Gutter: 12   points

New Document Preset Resolutions

Print Resolution: 300   pixels/inch

Screen Resolution: 72   pixels/inch

Figure 2-16: Selecting a ruler.

The following list describes the Units & Rulers options:

✦ **Rulers:** Rulers are displayed in inches by default, which is fine unless you're measuring in pixels for an image to be displayed on the Web.

Instead of constantly going to this drop-down list and choosing Pixels, try this:

a. *Press Ctrl+Shift+R to display rulers on the edges of the current image window.*

All new and opened documents now show rulers, so remember to turn off rulers when you're done.

b. *Right-click a ruler and then choose your measure of choice from the contextual menu.*

If you choose pixels, for example, bang! You're measuring in pixels.

✦ **Type:** Text is traditionally measured in points, and there's probably no reason to change the default setting in this menu.

✦ **Print Sizes:** By default, the Print Sizes preference is set to inches, which is fine.

If you need to use the metric system, specify mm or cm here.

✦ **Column and gutter sizes:** Column sizes aren't important unless you're composing an image for a desktop publishing layout. If that's the case, measure the space for the graphic or photo in the desktop publishing program and then enter the values in the Width and Gutter text boxes.

✦ **New Document Preset Resolutions:** The default for the Print Resolution text box and drop-down list, 300 pixels per inch (ppi), is a tad high. (Print houses use print resolutions of 240–266 ppi; Adobe rounds up the number up to make it easier to remember.) If you're editing an image to be displayed onscreen, the Screen Resolution default of 72 is fine and you shouldn't change it. This resolution is used by every application except Microsoft applications, which use 96 ppi resolution.

Grid Preferences

Click the Next button or choose Grid from the top drop-down list in the Preferences dialog box to see the options for grids.

A grid is nice when you're laying out a page (Web or otherwise).

When you choose Grid from the top drop-down list in the Preferences dialog box, you see the options for the display of the grid. You can set the grid's

✦ **Color:** Choose a color from the Color drop-down list.

Choose a color that contrasts with the predominant colors in the current image in the workspace. I usually select Light Red, as shown in Figure 2-17, because I do lots of outdoor photography and light red is almost never found in nature scenes.

Grid		
Color:	■ Light Red	⌄
Style:	Lines	⌄
Gridline every:	50	percent ⌄
Subdivisions:	1	

Figure 2-17: Set grid options here.

✦ **Type:** Choose from the Style drop-down list; lines, dashed lines, and dots are your options. (You cannot vary the width of grid lines.)

Choose Percent from the Gridline Every drop-down list. It's the most intuitive choice because people describe image areas in percentages — the lower-right quarter, the left half of a photo — you know. You usually don't know how large a new document will be. (Pressing Ctrl+K brings you back to the Preferences dialog box if you need to change the grid measurements to pixels or inches.)

You can also set up subdivisions for the grid; if you enter a value of 1 in the Subdivisions text box, no subdivisions appear (refer to Figure 2-17). You can toggle grid display on and off by choosing View➪Grid.

Plug-Ins & Scratch Disks Preferences

Click the Next button or choose Plug-Ins & Scratch Disks from the top drop-down list in the Preferences dialog box to see the options for plug-ins and scratch disks. (The Plug-ins folder is explained on page 67.)

This preference area has the most important choice you have to set up: where Elements write temp files: your *scratch disk.* Follow these guidelines to make sure that Elements has enough temporary space to work quickly and with stability:

✦ Choose a drive or two with lots of space. Elements writes multiple saved states of the image you're editing to these drives so you can undo mistakes. Don't worry; you'll probably never see these temp files, and Elements deletes them when you close the program.

✦ Don't specify your C: drive, unless you have only one drive. Every application on Earth installs to C:. Adobe calls it your *Startup drive;* see Figure 2-18.

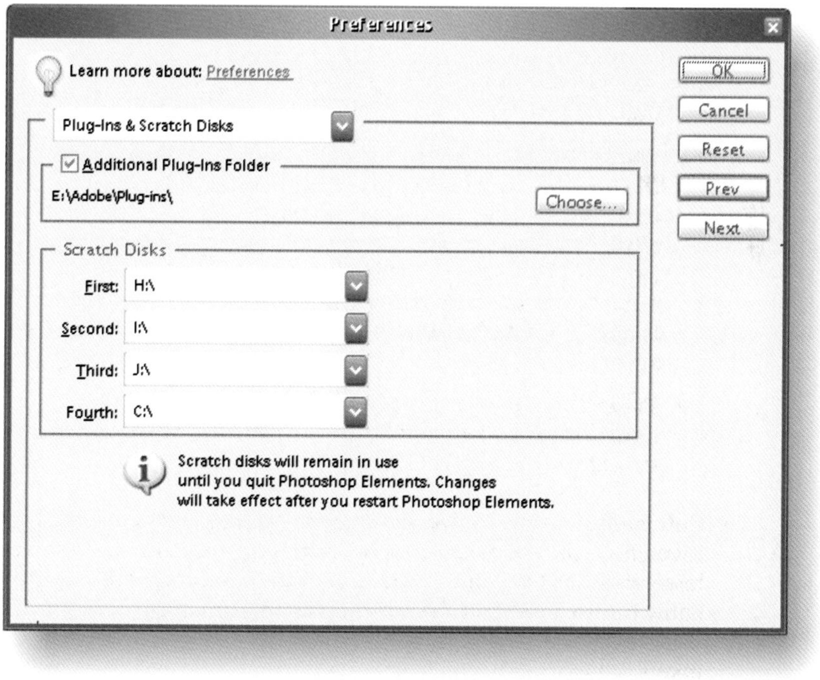

Figure 2-18: Specify where your scratch disk should live.

Memory & Image Cache Preferences

Click the Next button or choose Memory & Image Cache from the top drop-down list in the Preferences dialog box to see the options for memory and image cache preferences.

How much memory you allocate to Elements is critical to its performance. Try setting this preference at 75% and avoid running other programs while you run Elements. Elements does indeed work magic with images, but that magic comes at a price. The typical PCs that folks buy at their local Big Box Computer Warehouse, for example, come with 256MB of RAM — 75 percent of 256 is 192 (MB), which is the minimum amount to keep Elements happy. See Figure 2-19. I recommend that your computer has 500MB–1GB of RAM to run Elements and other of today's RAM-hungry applications.

Windows keeps a chunk of RAM in reserve for operating and disk management. Even if you were to crank the Elements memory usage up to the max of 100% *(don't do this!)*, Windows still keeps about 20 percent of total RAM in reserve.

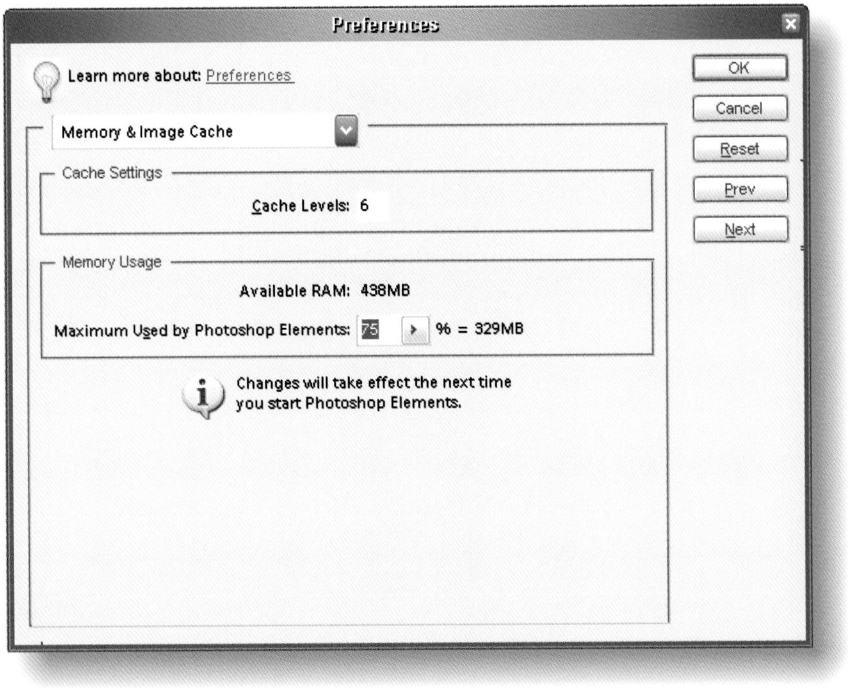

Preferences

Learn more about: Preferences

Memory & Image Cache

Cache Settings

Cache Levels: 6

Memory Usage

Available RAM: 438MB

Maximum Used by Photoshop Elements: 75 ▸ % = 329MB

OK
Cancel
Reset
Prev
Next

ⓘ Changes will take effect the next time you start Photoshop Elements.

Figure 2-19: Reserve some space for RAM.

Buy more RAM; it's cheap these days, and your nerdy nephew can install it.

Image cache speeds up reloading recent files by storing image data in your computer's memory. The default of 6 Levels usually strikes a healthy balance between

✦ No cache (recently opened/edited images take a while to load)

✦ Too much caching (which slows down your machine)

Type Preferences

Click the Next button or choose Type from the top drop-down list in the Preferences dialog box to see the options for type preferences (see Figure 2-20). Type preferences affect the way apostrophes are entered in a string of text, how vertical spacing is displayed, and how font previews are displayed on the Options bar.

```
                          Preferences                              ☒

  💡  Learn more about: Preferences                              ┌──────────┐
                                                                │    OK    │
  ┌────────────────────────────────┐                           └──────────┘
  │ Type                       ▼   │                           ┌──────────┐
  └────────────────────────────────┘                           │  Cancel  │
   ┌─ Type Options ──────────────────                          └──────────┘
   │  ☑ Use Smart Quotes                                       ┌──────────┐
   │  ☑ Show Asian Text Options                                │  Reset   │
   │  ☑ Show Font Names in English                             └──────────┘
   │  ☑ Font Preview Size:  Large  ▼                           ┌──────────┐
                                                                │   Prev   │
                                                                └──────────┘
                                                                ┌──────────┐
                                                                │   Next   │
                                                                └──────────┘
```

Figure 2-20: Select type preferences.

✦ **Use Smart Quotes:** Smart quotes are typesetter's quotes, also known as curly quotes. They lend a touch of professionalism in your work without having to look up the key codes in the Windows Character Map utility.

✦ **Show Asian Text Options:**

- If you work in an Asian language, mark this check box.

- If you use vertical text frequently and want to adjust the spacing between characters, mark this check box. (Read more about this topic in Book VII, Chapter 1.)

✦ **Show Font Names in English:** Many of the bigger, better type foundries are in Germany. If you want a font named *Kunstlerschreibsch* to appear in the Type list on the Options bar, leave this box blank. Otherwise, an easier-to-read *Kunstler Script* appears when you check this box.

✦ **Font Preview Size:** I recommend choosing Large from this drop-down list. Chances are that you're running a 1024 x 768 display; at that screen resolution, the fonts appear too tiny to appreciate on the Options bar drop-down list when you choose a Type tool. See Figure 2-21.

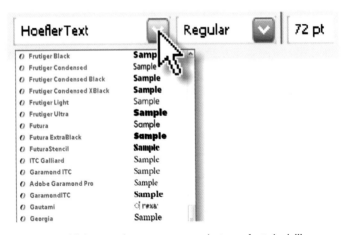

Figure 2-21: Make sure that you can see what your fonts look like.

You're done setting preferences! You can choose Organize and Share from the Preferences drop-down list, but this takes you to the Organizer, which I cover in Chapter 1 of this mini-book.

The ins and outs of plug-ins

Plug-ins are mini-applications, designed by independent programmers, that you use to extend the Elements features and effects. You don't have to install a third-party plug-in in the Elements plug-ins folder, which is welcome news if you have multiple hard drive partitions and the partition on which you installed Elements is crowded. You install these plug-ins in a unique folder on a hard drive and then use the Preferences dialog box to direct Elements to this folder.

Almost every third-party plug-in that's designed for Photoshop also works in Elements. (On your next payday, you might want to pick up the Flaming Pear Flood filter or the Alien Skin Eye Candy suite.)

Many bitmap programs and some vector design programs, such as Xara Xtreme and Painter, use Adobe standard plug-ins. You don't need to install a plug-in twice — they're available on the Filters menu after you restart Elements.

The Image menu

In the Image menu (see Figure 2-22), you can perform some extremely simple — and one or two more-complex — image editing moves.

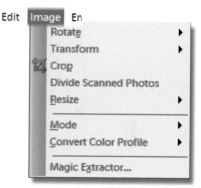

Figure 2-22: The Image menu.

✦ **Rotate:** The Rotate menu item contains submenus. You can rotate or *flip* (mirror) a regular image or an image layer (without affecting the other image layers).

I don't recommend the Straighten Photo command (it doesn't work with most images). Straighten a picture by using the Straighten tool on the Toolbox — which I cover in Book VI, Chapter 1.

✦ **Transform:** The Transform controls are more easily accessed and applied by pressing Ctrl+T when a layer (but not the image background) is chosen on the Layers palette. See Book IV, Chapter 4 for more information on rotating, skewing, scaling, and distorting image areas.

+ **Crop:** Use the Crop command when you have an area selected in an image. The area can be a rectangular, oval, or freeform shape. Elements crops to the selection's outermost edges.

  The Crop tool isn't the same as the Crop command. See more info on the Crop tool, later in this chapter.

+ **Resize:** Resizing can be more easily accomplished by right-clicking an image window title bar and choosing whether you want to

  - *Resize* (resample) the image by using the Image Size command (increasing or decreasing dimensions while keeping image resolution and thus changing the photo's pixel structure — its physical content).

  - *Change the image resolution without changing its physical content* (also performed using the Image Size command). Clear the Resample check box; as you increase the amount in the Resolution field, the dimensions of the image decrease.

  - *Change the Canvas Size* (which only crops or expands the image window and doesn't touch the size or color of the pixels in the image).

+ **Mode:** A more appropriate name for this command would be *Color Depth.* The pixels in a bitmap image have a range of color capability.

  - **RGB color.** For example, a 24-bit image means that 16.7 million unique colors can exist in the image, which is darned photorealistic. By default, all new Elements images and your digital camera's JPEG images are created in RGB mode. An 8-bit green, an 8-bit blue, and an 8-bit red color channel combine to make up RGB images.

  - **Grayscale** allows only 256 unique shades of black to be displayed.

  - **Indexed color** images can hold only 256 colors, like Grayscale mode images (although Grayscale is a special mode), and Indexed color images, such as GIFs, are called *8-bit images.*

  - **Bitmap** mode is only 1-bit deep; only black or white makes up such an image. You don't create an image in Bitmap or Indexed color; instead, you decrease an RGB or Grayscale image to these modes.

To prevent images from looking totally hideous at shallow color depths, Elements offers diffusion dithering. *Dithering* is the intelligent placement of different colored pixels near each other so when the image is viewed at a distance, it looks okay although not as good as an RGB image. The reason for Indexed color mode is that the GIF file format can hold only 256 unique colors; computer graphics basically started with GIF because of comparatively primitive technology in the late 1980s. And you can't create a GIF animation without dithering a copy of the RGB image down to Indexed color. Grayscale images print to laser printers with no unexpected image irregularities that you might encounter printing an RGB image, and Bitmap mode also prints to low-resolution laser jet printers acceptably.

Figure 2-23 shows close-ups of Indexed and Bitmap images; lower color capability equals smaller saved images but less image fidelity, so experiment with these color modes only on *copies* of your work. I reduced an RGB image to 16 colors instead of 256 (which looks much better) to show you a very visible example of color dithering.

Indexed color   Bitmap

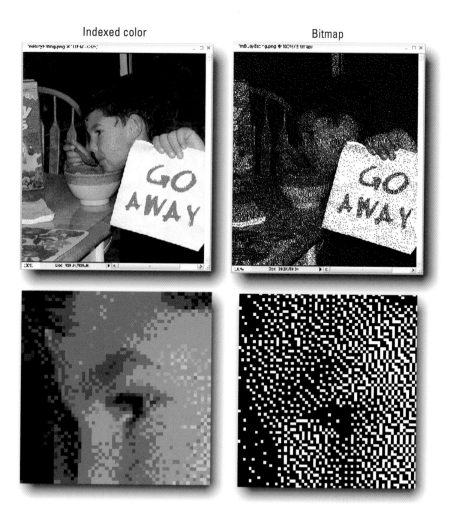

Figure 2-23: Indexed and bitmap images.

By default, a new image exists in 8-bit RGB color mode, supported by PSD, TIFF, PNG, JPEG, and a few other file formats. New digital cameras save images to 32-bit (usually in the Raw file format, which I cover in Book II), and expensive scanners can sample to 48 bits: I'm talking a color capacity of *billions* of colors. If you have a hi-fi image such as these, do your editing work and then save a copy to PNG, TIFF, or PSD in 8-bit mode.

✦ The **Color Table** command shows the colors used in Indexed mode images (GIFs). And you can reassign a color in the image by clicking its swatch, which usually makes the image look horrid. You can also load or choose a Custom color table to remap it to look like a psychedelic poster from the 1960s, but this is all peanuts compared with editing using Quick Fix, Levels, or Hue/Saturation. Most editing tools are disabled with Indexed color images.

✦ **Convert Color Profile:** This command is used for converting an sRGB-profiled image to Adobe RGB (and vice versa if you want to shrink the color space and clip out unique tones). Changing color profiles doesn't affect the image's color mode or saved file size.

✦ **Magic Extractor:** This works only on Grayscale and RGB mode images. It's a semi-automated way of separating an image's foreground subject from its background — see Book IV, Chapter 2.

The Enhance menu

The Enhance menu (see Figure 1-24) has two main groups: the Auto commands and the Adjust commands. In addition, there are really only four Enhance menu items that don't have shortcuts in the workspace yet can significantly advance your work: Levels, Hue/Saturation, Defringe, and Variations, all of which are located on submenus.

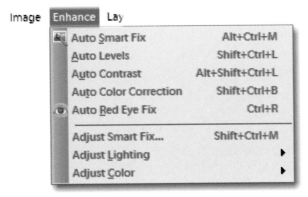

Figure 2-24: Dig down to find important options on the Enhance menu.

The Auto commands

The Auto Smart Fix, Auto Levels, Auto Contrast, Auto Color Correction, and Auto Red Eye Fix commands are all "one-pop" deals: You click the command, the command is executed, and it has no options. The Adjust Smart Fix command enables you to set the Smart Fixing amount before you use Auto Smart Fix. Because you cannot adjust the Auto settings, I suggest that you use the controls in Smart Fix mode (covered in Book I, Chapter 3) rather than these commands.

The Levels command

By choosing Enhance⇨Adjust Lighting (or pressing Ctrl+L — it's easier), you can adjust the brightness values in an image in three areas: Shadows (by using the Black Point slider), midtones (the middle slider on the top strip), and the image's highlights (by using the White Point slider). The Input area is used to increase image contrast; the midpoint slider reduces or increases midrange contrast by dragging it left or right. The output field sliders are used to decrease image contrast. If only an area of an image needs tone work, first use a selection tool to isolate the problem area, right-click and choose Feather to make a soft selection (so your edits don't come out with a hard edge), press Ctrl+L, and do your adjusting. See Book IV, Chapter 1 for detailed info on creating selections and feathering them.

I show you how to use the Levels command in Book III, Chapter 1. Manual tuning of tones (not colors) is better performed by eye than by letting Elements perform guesswork via the Auto buttons in several command boxes.

 Although Levels adjusts only brightness values (tones) and doesn't touch the colors (Hue), Levels can draw out the Saturation, or the amount of color. I routinely visit the Hue/Saturation feature (Ctrl+U) directly after applying the Levels command to decrease saturation.

The Adjust Hue/Saturation command

Found under Adjust Color, Hue/Saturation (Ctrl+U) is a useful command, used in many examples in this book. You can see three characteristics in a color, and this command enables you to adjust each one independently of the others:

✦ *Hue* is the predominant color in an area; red is a warm hue as it relates to photography, and the blue hues in the visible spectrum are cold. Thus, color casting can be corrected by using the Hue slider.

✦ *Saturation* is the distinctiveness of a hue — how much pure color is in an area versus how much gray is present. An orange Popsicle and household cleanser packaging use much saturation, but text on a page is usually not saturated at all.

✦ *Lightness* is sort of akin to the terms brightness and luminosity; it's the amount of white blended into a photo.

If you have an image whose tones are muddy or faint, press Ctrl+L to use the Levels command on such an image rather than the Hue/Saturation Lightness slider.

The Adjust Color⇨Adjust Color for Skin Tone command adjusts the entire image, not just a person's skin, and this command messes with images that don't even contain people or skin. Instead, use the Quick Fix mode's Temperature and Tint controls on a selection of a person's face if the person appears too blue or too red.

The Defringe Layer command

Found off the Adjust Color menu, the Defringe Layer command is very useful. As its name indicates, it works only on layers.

Fringing (a sort of halo) can occur at the edge of an object on a transparent layer in

✦ The background of selected content similar in color to the foreground object

✦ Image areas that feature diffuse, random, small, and natural objects (such as a person with really kinky hair, or a complex outline of treetops)

Defringe replaces these unwanted edge pixel colors with colors detected inside the object area (see Figure 2-25). Usually a value of 1 in the Defringe dialog box remedies layer fringing.

Figure 2-25: The result of working with the useful Defringe Layer command.

The Color Variations command

Color Variations presents you with a dialog box that offers a lot of control over image color casting. Found under the Adjust Color command, it's pretty intuitive to use (and covered in Book III, Chapter 2). Follow these steps to warm up a cold image or to chill out a warm photo:

1. **Adjust the amount of color change you propose to apply with the Amount slider.**

   Control the amount of adjusting with the Amount slider first, not second as the text in the dialog box suggests. Less is more. If you drag the Amount slider all the way to the left, you get no variations; conversely, dragging this slider all the way to the right gives you wild variations in color, which isn't useful. Because the Amount slider has no tick marks, I suggest that you set it to the first or second "tugs" from the far-left side — you might notice your cursor resisting movement at intervals. Choose the first or second resistance point.

2. **Choose a tonal range — Highlights, Midtones (where much visual information usually resides in photos), or Shadows.**

3. **Click a preview box that addresses the image's defect.**

If the image is too warm, cool it down by choosing less blue. Here's the effect of the Color Variations choices:

✦ Blue is the color opposite of yellow, so pick Increase Blue if your photo is too warm.

✦ Green is the color opposite of magenta (old photos frequently age to a magenta color cast), so pick Increase Green to do photo restoration.

✦ Red is the color opposite cyan, so pick Increase Red to warm up a picture.

   You can click any Variations preview more than once to add or subtract color settings, and the blue, green, and red controls blend with one another — you often need to choose from more than one color preview.

Because you have Saturation control in Variations, you can use this command to decrease an image's intensity without a visit to the Hue/Saturation command afterward.

The Layer menu

On the Layer menu, you can find the New, Duplicate Layer, and Delete Layer commands that you use to create and remove layers in a layered composition; see Figure 2-26.

These commands are more easily executed by working the controls directly on the Layers palette, covered in Book V, Chapter 1.

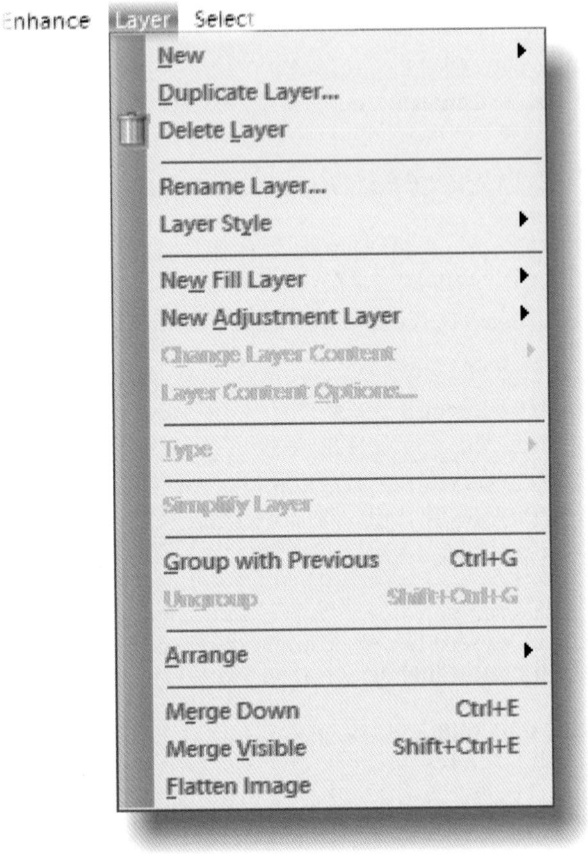

Enhance Layer Select

New ▶
Duplicate Layer...
Delete Layer

Rename Layer...
Layer Style ▶

New Fill Layer ▶
New Adjustment Layer ▶
Change Layer Content ▶
Layer Content Options...

Type ▶

Simplify Layer

Group with Previous   Ctrl+G
Ungroup   Shift+Ctrl+G

Arrange ▶

Merge Down   Ctrl+E
Merge Visible   Shift+Ctrl+E
Flatten Image

Figure 2-26: Working with layers in a composition.

TIP

The easy way to rename a layer is to double-click its name on the Layers palette and then type a layer's title on the Layers palette. Layer names can be the same, with no practical length limit to a layer name.

To continue down the Layer menu list:

✦ **Layer Style:** Layer Style is active only when a Style is applied to a layer by using the Styles and Effects palette, as covered in Book V, Chapter 1.

✦ **New Fill Layer:** New Fill Layer is a quick way to create a new layer and fill it with a solid color, a gradient, or a saved or preset pattern. However, you can do all these tasks manually, and this command has no option for setting the start or end point of a gradient, as you can do manually. (See Chapter 3 of this mini-book.)

✦ **New Adjustment Layer:** Accessing New Adjustment Layer is more quickly accomplished by clicking the "Moon Pie" cookie icon on the Layers palette. Adjustment layers are explained in Book V, Chapter 2.

✦ **Change Layer Content:** Change Layer Content is available only for Adjustment layers in compositions.

✦ **Layer Content Options:** These apply only to the (Adjustment) Layer content.

✦ **Type:** All the options for text can be more easily used from the Options bar when a Type tool is selected (see Book VII, Chapter 1).

✦ **Simplify Layer:** This command does two things:

- Reduces Styles and Effects to base pixels that you can then edit

- Converts text you type to pixels for editing purposes

Text in Elements is based on vector outlines, so the Elements bitmap paint tools cannot be used until the vectors are simplified into pixels.

You can also simplify layer content by right-clicking a layer thumbnail on the Layers palette and then choosing Simplify from the contextual menu.

Grouping and ungrouping layers (Group with Previous and Ungroup commands) is useful for hiding and unhiding multiple layers using the eye icon on the Layers palette. Linking layers isn't the same as grouping layers.

To link layers, hold Shift and then click more than one layer on the Layers palette. Linking is the key to scaling, rotating, and performing other transformations to several layers at a time. You unlink layers by clicking a linked layer; the layer becomes unlinked and is then the chosen layer to edit.

Continuing down the Layer menu list

✦ **Arrange:** The Arrange commands are more easily performed by dragging Layers palette thumbnails up or down.

✦ **Merge Down:** Merge Down (Ctrl+E) merges the current working image layer with the layer directly underneath. If you have a hidden layer underneath the layer you want to merge down, the command doesn't work, and you need to rearrange the order of the visible layers to the downward merge.

✦ **Merge Visible:** Merge Visible blends all visible layers to the background layer, and hidden layers move to the top of the layer stack.

The Select menu

Selections are sort of a relic technology — it's far more intuitive to work with selected image areas on layers. You can save selections to PSD, TIFF, and Targa file formats.

Selecting all (Select⇨All) is more easily done by pressing Ctrl+A. The short-cut to deselect is Ctrl+D.

TIP

If a chum of yours owns Photoshop CS and passes along to you a TIFF image with a saved selection, the selection is named Alpha 1, by default. Although Photoshop can save entire grayscale images as a selection (often called an *alpha channel*), Elements doesn't have this feature.

Continuing down the Select menu, you can find these commands:

✦ **Inverse:** Choosing Select⇨Inverse requires that you have created a selection on the background image or on a layer. To invert a selection, just press Ctrl+Shift+I; then, all selected areas are protected from editing (they're masked), and other areas are selected.

✦ **Select All Layers:** Using Select All Layers is actually linking layers.

To select multiple layers manually, Shift-click layer thumbnails on the Layers palette.

✦ **Feathering:** Feathering is performed on a selection to soften the selection so that when you cut or copy the image area beneath the selection, a transition is made at the selection edge between full opacity inside the edge to transparency outside the edge (see Figure 2-27).

Figure 2-27: Soften things up with the feathering effect.

Feathering is a great way to frame images and create a soft edge. However, don't confuse feathering with blurring an image edge or image content. Feathering changes the edge opacity, without blurring the center. Blurring changes the overall image focus. When you right-click a selection using a selection tool, you can access the Feather command.

You can't perform feathering after choosing Select⇨All because the feathering can't grow outside of the window border.

✦ **Modify:** The Modify commands are quite useful. You use this group to change the shape of a selection:

- **Expand** changes the current selection to include more image area, but retains the selection shape.

- **Contract** makes the selection smaller. There is a limit to contracting a selection — you can't contract by a value greater than the size of the selection.

- **Smooth** rounds the corners on a rectangular selection, but without feathering. Smoothing selections made with the Lasso tools can help the overall accuracy of the selection, softening corner points and virtually eliminating jaggy selection actions made accidentally.

- **Border** creates a tube out of a selection, great for painting into the selection to create outlines.

  Unlike the Edit⇨Stroke selection command, Border feathers the new selection, and there is no option to turn off the feathering.

✦ **Grow:** The Grow command expands the selection to include either

- Objects on a layer

- Areas of similar color on the Background layer

Grow isn't totally predictable. You might need to use the Selection Brush in Mask mode to refine the Grow selection.

✦ **Similar Select:** The Similar Select command is useful for selecting by image color and not by geometry. Just select an image area's color (use the Magic Wand tool for precise selection and the Lasso tool for broader color areas); then choose the Similar command. Areas of similar hue and saturation are selected. (Tools are covered in Chapter 3 of this mini-book.)

✦ **Saving Selections:** Saving Selections, an action whereby an image area is saved to an invisible area within the image file, isn't the same as copying or cutting a selection to a layer. Saved selections contain no image detail info. A selection can be saved and then loaded that contains only the geometry and opacity. Opacity reflects the amount of selectedness; this is done by

a. *Painting with a brush with partial opacity set on the Options bar.*

b. *Loading a selection by Ctrl-clicking the layer's thumbnail and then saving the selection.*

You can view only a loaded selection's *marquee* (the animated dashes onscreen); you cannot see a saved selection. Saved selections of less than 50% can be loaded and used and edited, but no marquee will appear onscreen.

The Filter menu

Filters are mini-applications used to distort, sharpen, or perform other modifications to an image or a selected image area. Also called *plug-ins,* filters can liven up compositions and correct image areas, and are part of the power of Elements.

You can use filters to export to special file formats, such as third-party accessories like CyberMesh and Genuine Fractals, whose commands appear when you choose File➪Export, not the Filter menu.

Many Elements filters can be accessed by double-clicking an icon in the Styles and Effects palette's Filters collection (see Figure 2-28).

The View menu

You use the View menu commands to choose how you view your work (see Figure 2-29).

Three commands here can be accomplished by using tools or keyboard shortcuts:

✦ **Zoom In/Zoom Out:** Press Ctrl++ (the plus key)/ Ctrl+– (the minus key), respectively.

✦ **Fit on Screen:** Double-click the Hand tool.

✦ **Actual Size:** Double-click the Zoom tool.

Suppose that you're working close up on a fine detail in an image and you need to see how the overall image is shaping up. Call up one or more image windows and view the original in a zoomed-out screen resolution. In Figure 2-30, you can see two views of the same image.

These new view windows are of the *same* image:

✦ These new windows are updated while you edit in the main window (unlike choosing the File➪Duplicate command).

✦ You can close new view windows at any time without losing your work.

✦ You can edit in any New View window.

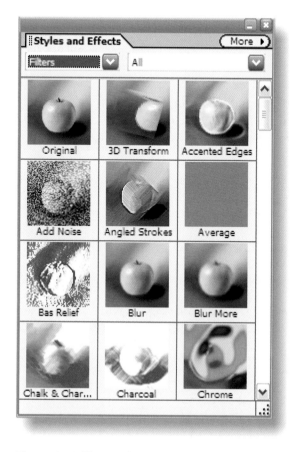

Figure 2-28: Elements has an abundance of Filters options.

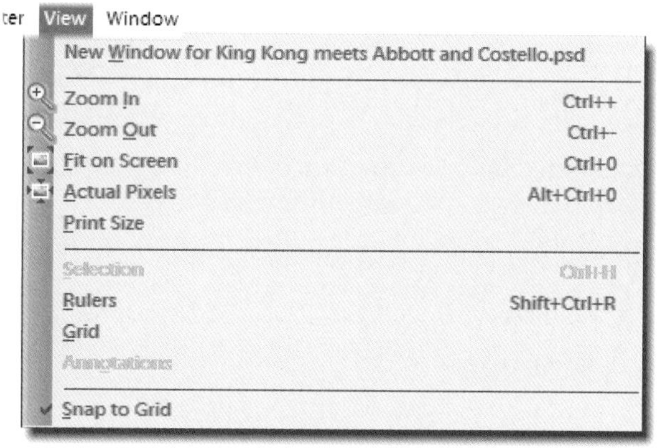

ter **View** Window

New Window for King Kong meets Abbott and Costello.psd	
Zoom In	Ctrl++
Zoom Out	Ctrl+-
Fit on Screen	Ctrl+0
Actual Pixels	Alt+Ctrl+0
Print Size	
Selection	Ctrl+H
Rulers	Shift+Ctrl+R
Grid	
Annotations	
✓ Snap to Grid	

Figure 2-29: Viewing the View menu.

Figure 2-30: The New View window enables you to edit at different viewing resolutions without using the Zoom tool.

✦ When you save the main window (File➪Save), you save everything.

✦ New View windows can be closed without saving because there's nothing different to save.

Moving down on the View menu, you find controls for displaying grid lines and rulers in an image window:

✦ Rulers are easily displayed by pressing Ctrl+Shift+R. See the preceding section for ruler preferences. (Myself, I preferred King George as a ruler.)

✦ Grid requires the View➪Grid command to become visible; see the earlier Preferences section for Grid setup suggestions.

✦ Snap to Grid is a welcome command when you want to align images on different layers.

The Window menu

Elements uses standard Windows commands for tiling and cascading image windows.

The Toolbox can be toggled on and off by the Tools command. Without tools displayed, though, image editing is harder.

Much of the Windows menu is devoted to the display of palettes. You'll use palettes frequently in image editing; the following Windows commands are in the following list (including shortcut keys, if available):

+ **Colors swatches palette:** This has no shortcut key.

+ **How To (F6):** This collection of steps and tips for performing tasks ranges from ho-hum to inspired.

+ **Styles and Effects palette (F7):** I think it's better to keep this palette stowed in the Palette Bin.

+ **Info palette (F8):** This is a good resource for measuring selections.

+ **Navigator palette (F12):** This is a waste of workspace after you learn to use the Zoom and Hand tools.

+ **Undo History palette:** This has no keyboard shortcut.

If you feel you're prone to mistakes, keep this palette in the Palette Bin or attach it to a floating palette. (See how to do this in the upcoming section, "The Elements Tear-off Elements.")

+ **Undo History palette:** Use this to scroll up or down to various states in your image editing. The number of available states is determined in General Preferences, which you can read about earlier in this chapter.

In Figure 2-31, I goofed up when adding a Shadows/Highlights edit. To correct my errant ways, I dragged the arrow icon on the left side of the list up to the previous command — the one before I used the Enhance⇨ Adjust Lighting⇨Shadows/Highlights command.

Every menu command (and painting and other editing moves that use Toolbox tools) is recorded on the Undo History palette, and this palette is way easier than pressing Ctrl+Z or Ctrl+Y *ad nauseum*.

Undo steps are *sequential* — you can't skip a step going forward or backward.

The Help menu

This menu is fairly self-explanatory.

You need an active Internet connection to access such features as online help.

Figure 2-31: The Undo History palette provides a convenient way to review and undo your image editing.

The Elements Tear-off Elements

I'm not a big believer in scrolling all over town to access a command or feature, so I like to keep my artist's materials close to the image window. So can you.

Detaching the Toolbox

In Figure 2-32, I detached the Toolbox from its docked position by dragging on the dotted line at its top.

When you undock the Toolbox, it's reconfigured to two columns. (You can't change the number of columns.) This configuration is easier to choose tools from because when the Toolbox is undocked

✦ You can drag it close to your image window to edit more quickly.

✦ You can reattach it — drag it by its top to its original docking position.

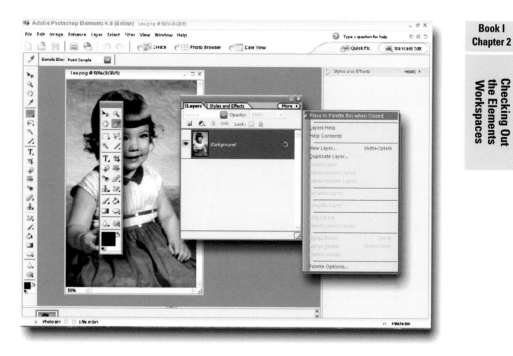

Figure 2-32: Float your editing tools for easy access and to gain screen real estate.

Configuring palettes

Palettes are another screen element you can reconfigure; you can drag them from the Palette Bin and group them to suit your work habits:

+ Palettes can be dragged off the Palette Bin and positioned next to your work. I used the Layers palette as a floating window.

+ You can group palettes by dragging them on top of one another.

You gain advantages when you customize your workspace by grouping and floating palettes:

+ Group together Layers, Styles and Effects, and the Info palette. These palettes are the ones you use most in editing.

+ With a palette group floating, you can close the Palette Bin from the Window menu to gain at least 20 percent of screen space for images.

In Figure 2-33, you can see a palette group and a floating Toolbox.

Figure 2-33: Grouping and floating Elements tools makes accessing the tools more convenient.

To ungroup a palette, follow these steps:

1. **Click its tab.**
2. **Click More.**
3. **Choose Place in Palette Bin When Closed.**
4. **Drag it by the tab off the palette group.**

Chapter 3: The Toolbox, Options, and Other Essential Stuff

In This Chapter

✏ **Using the power behind all the brush tip options**

✏ **Creating your own, elegant brush tip**

✏ **Using the Color Replacement brush to tint an image**

✏ **Using Paint Bucket to fill with patterns**

✏ **Creating your own color gradient**

The Toolbox in Elements deserves a thorough examination, as do a couple of other items you often use. Think of this chapter as an extension of the preceding chapter; it's impossible to document the entire Elements interface in a single chapter. In this chapter, you find out how to create and apply patterns, make a metallic fill, replace certain colors in your photos, and do lots of good stuff for image editing — and you're in Book I! Imagine what you can do after you lift off from this necessary but exciting foundation work.

You can find all the files I use in this chapter at www.dummies.com/go/PhotoshopElementsAIOFD1e.

Exploring The Toolbox

The Toolbox consists of three types of tools, which are not arranged in order or groups: painting tools, selection tools, and tools for adjusting an image area's *tones* (its brightness values) and focus. Figure 3-1 shows you all the tools.

Enable Tool Tips in General Preferences (press Ctrl+K). Then, when you hover your cursor over a tool, you can see its name and keyboard shortcut. (In my opinion, though, it's not worthwhile to memorize more than L for the Lasso tools and M for the Marquee tools.)

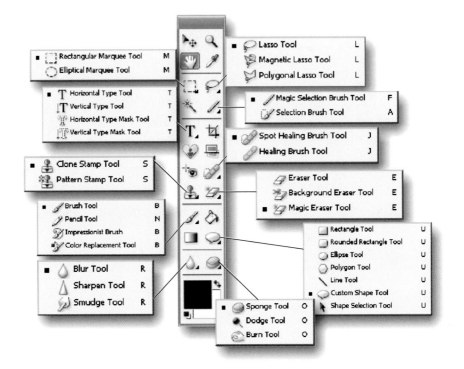

Figure 3-1: The Toolbox holds, well, lots of tools.

The selection tools are the key to sophisticated image editing; I cover them in depth in Book IV.

The Move tool is not a selection tool. Selections are inert: They cannot do anything to the image below it. The Move tool (the top tool on the Toolbox), on the other hand, is used exclusively to

✦ Move a selection and the image area beneath it

✦ Move unselected image areas copied or cut to a layer

✦ Distort selections and image areas — called *free-transforming* an area — which I cover in Book VIII, Chapter 2

Discovering the Painting Tools

You primarily find painting tools useful for creating patterns and backgrounds; a retouched photo often looks phony if you paint within image areas.

In this section, I take you through the obvious (and not so obvious) uses for the painting tools. Figure 3-2 shows you the group of painting tools of the Toolbox.

✎ Brush Tool		B
▪ ✎ Pencil Tool		N
✎ Impressionist Brush		B
▪✎ Color Replacement Tool		B

TIP

Whenever a tool icon has a tick mark to its lower-right corner, more tools are tucked underneath. Just click-drag to reveal the additional tools.

Figure 3-2: Use the Elements paint tools when you don't need image retouching.

Getting colors to paint with is obviously a must. Although you can click colors from the Color Swatches palette (choose Window➪Color Swatches), just clicking the foreground color swatch from the Toolbox is far easier (see Figure 3-3). This action takes you to the *Color Picker,* where you can choose a shade with which to paint. The *background color* swatch is the color you erase to, and these colors can be swapped by clicking the double-headed arrow icon or by pressing the X key.

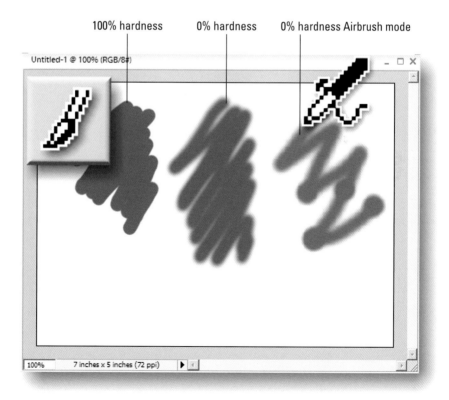

100% hardness   0% hardness   0% hardness Airbrush mode

Untitled-1 @ 100% (RGB/8#)

100%   7 inches x 5 inches (72 ppi)

Figure 3-3: The paint-specifying controls in the Elements Toolbox.

You can paint with black and erase to white by clicking the Default colors icon (or by pressing D).

Use the Eyedropper tool (refer to Figure 3-3) to *sample* — to select and then use — colors in an image. Just click over an area, and the exact color appears on the face of the foreground swatch. Sampling colors is often better than whipping one up in the Color Picker; the human eye prefers brilliant and stimulating (and often, unrealistic) colors when painted into a photo. Press Alt-click with the Eyedropper, and the sampled color becomes the background swatch.

By pressing X regularly as you work, you've got a palette of two colors immediately at your disposal.

The Brush tool group

The painting tool group consists of the Brush tool (of the tools in the group, you use this one the most), the Pencil, the Color Replacement tool, and the Impressionist Brush tool.

Each tool has options that modify how it applies color, which I show in the following sections.

The Brush tool

Use the Brush tool to apply foreground color. You adjust the *opacity* (the percentage mixed on the canvas) of the foreground color that you apply from the Options bar, which reflects the options for the chosen tool along with the size of the brush tip, the hardness, and the painting mode (such as Multiply or Screen).

You can read more about painting modes in Book V, Chapter 3.

Try out the following steps to get a handle — get it, *handle?* — on the basic Brush tool options:

1. **Ctrl+double-click the workspace (or choose File⇨New).**

2. **In the Preset field in the New dialog box, choose Default Photoshop Elements Size and then press Enter.**

3. **Choose the Brush tool from the Toolbox, click the foreground color swatch, choose a color, and then press Enter.**

   In this example, I opted for a bright blue.

4. **Right-click over the image to display the Default Brushes tips.**

You don't have to mouse all the way up to the Options bar to pick a tip.

5. Choose a tip and make a scribble.

I chose the 19 pixel hard tip. You can tell a hard tip from a soft one by its icon appearance: The hard tips are first in order on the palette, and the soft tips have a smeary little icon.

The brush strokes are smooth but crisp.

6. Choose a contrasting tip and make another scribble.

Right-click to bring up brush tip options. I chose the 21 pixel soft tip.

As you can see, the edges where you scribble are soft.

7. Click the Airbrush icon on the Options bar, click-hold on an area, and then stroke.

The paint spreads, just like the effect with an actual airbrush. See how it looks in Figure 3-4.

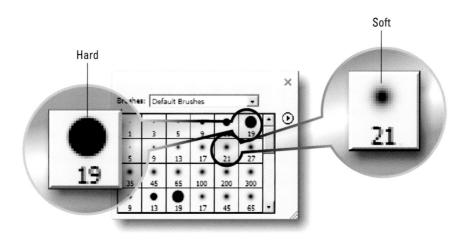

Figure 3-4: The Brush tool imitates many different real-life brushes.

You can achieve lots of looks by using the Brush tool. Click the paintbrush icon to the right of the More Options legend on the Options bar (see Figure 3-5). Some brush properties might seem obvious to you, but I explain them all, along with their purposefulness in your Elements work.

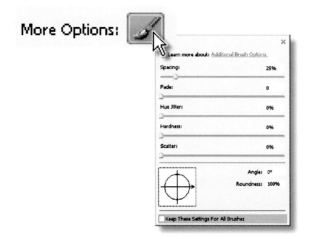

Figure 3-5: The More Options flyout palette.

Spacing

Think of a brush stroke as a single paint daub followed immediately by another daub. If you space the individual daubs, you get a dotted line — and this is precisely what the Spacing option is for.

✦ The default is 25%, which produces a seamless stroke — no dots.

✦ At 0%, you get a smooth (unbroken) stroke that's a little thicker than the 25% setting.

✦ At 100%, your strokes produce an image that looks like scattered billiard balls.

If you set the Spacing for a brush tip to 100%, you paint a dotted line, with each daub spaced from the next by 100% of the tip's diameter. For example, using a 19 pixel tip leaves a 19 pixel gap between the first and following daubs.

Try this feature:

1. **Click the More Options brush icon (at the right end of the Options bar) when a painting tool is chosen, drag the Spacing slider to 100%, and make a zig-zag stroke.**

2. **Click the Airbrush icon, click-hold, make a second zig-zag stroke, and then click-hold again.**

See Figure 3-6 for the results.

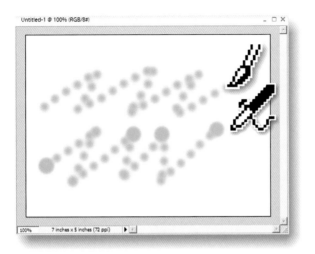

Figure 3-6: Use spacing to draw anything from road maps to Pac-Man power dots.

Hue Jitter and Scatter

Hue Jitter creates a transition between your chosen foreground and background colors when you make strokes. Scatter does exactly what its name implies: It makes dots of color randomly stray off the course of your stroke. Use the Hue Jitter slider to set different percentages; the following list highlights the effects of using different percentages:

✦ At 0%, the foreground color totally dominates — there is no effect.

✦ At 50%, some background color sneaks in.

✦ At 100%, you get in every stroke a fairly even mix of foreground blending into background color.

Hue Jitter is particularly effective when used in combination with the Scatter option, which I discuss a little later in this chapter. Try this example.

Hue Jitter doesn't cycle through all the colors of the rainbow; it just "jitters" between foreground and background colors. If you want to create a rainbow, use the Gradient tool, which I discuss in the upcoming section, "The Gradient tool."

If you use a digitizing tablet rather than a mouse, you can control the intensity of the brush options by applying stylus pressure. Just choose the Tablet Options field from the Options bar.

Creating Strokes with Hue Jitter and Scatter

Here's how to create strokes with Hue Jitter and Scatter.

1. **Choose a soft brush tip, set the foreground color to light purple, set the background to set the Hue Jitter to 100%, and draw a spiral.**

    You create an instant, exotic, wooly caterpillar, as shown in the figure here.

2. **Try using a larger soft tip with a red foreground and a green background, and stroke in one area.**

    You create an interesting mottled texture, as shown in the figure here.

3. **Humor me and choose purple as the foreground color and blue as the background color.**

4. **On the More Options flyout palette, set the Spacing to 50%, set the Scatter option to 50%, and then drag the Size slider on the Options bar to 7 pixels. (Click the triangle next to the number field to display the slider.)**

5. **Draw an X (lowercase or uppercase is fine). See the result in the figure.**

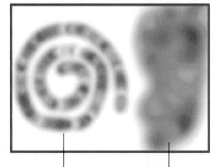

Hue Jitter (red to purple)

Hue Jitter (red to green)

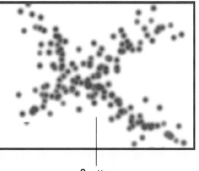

Scatter

Brush hardness

You're likely to run into plenty of design situations where the Default Brushes tip palette doesn't have the exact size or degree of hardness you want. No problem. Follow these steps to customize any size brush tip hardness:

1. **Choose the size tip by dragging the Size slider on the Options bar.**

2. **Choose the hardness by dragging the Hardness slider on the Brush Options flyout menu.**

For example, I've built (for my personal use) a 2 pixel, 80% hard tip, which I use for clone stamp work — image editing often calls for a 2 pixel tip. Clone stamping is covered in Book IX, Chapter 2, and I show you how to save a custom tip in the upcoming section, "Creating your own brush tip."

Tips can be accessed by using painting, toning, focusing, erasing, and cloning tools.

The Fade option

On the More Options palette, don't try to calculate the length of a fade with a brush; Elements calculates the *fade* — the distance between 100% opacity and 100% transparency in a stroke — by steps from 0 to 9999, combined with stroke spacing. Instead, just set an amount (35 is good for a medium-sized tip) and stroke; press Ctrl+Z to undo if you didn't hit the magic number, and then try again.

In Figure 3-7, you can see the result of setting Fade to 16 and then to 38. Then I added Hue Jitter and painted an amateurish fireworks display.

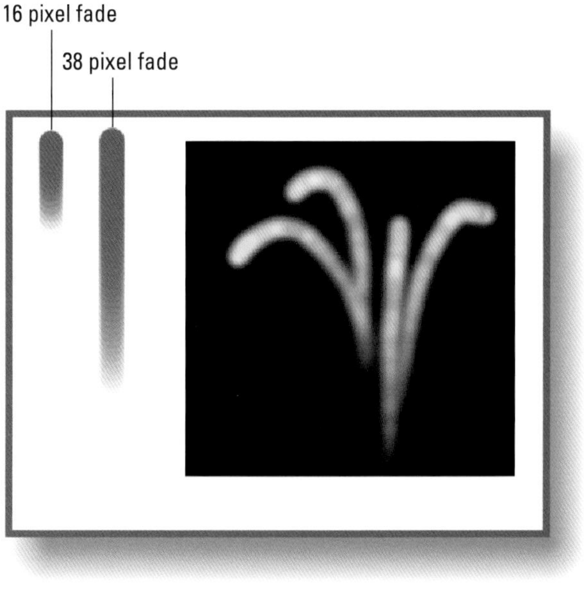

16 pixel fade

38 pixel fade

Figure 3-7: Fade makes a stroke transition from opacity to transparency.

Use Fade to suggest motion in cartoon work.

Brush angle and roundness

You're likely to run into retouching situations where you need to clone or erase into a cranny in an image area. (Read more about cloning in Book VI, Chapter 2.)

It's a royal pain to keep reducing brush size, so here's my workaround: Squash a brush tip into an oval and then set the angle you want.

Putting It Together

Painting with a Smooshed Brush Tip

Here are some painting exercises to familiarize you with the options:

1. **On the Brush Options flyout menu, click-drag one of the black dots next to the crosshair brush tip circle on the bottom of the flyout.**

2. **Drag the arrow atop the tip circle until the angle reads 45 degrees (or type** 45 **in the Angle number field).**

3. **Drag a zig-zag stroke and then stroke over the first stroke, by stroking down and up where the first stroke goes up and down.**

   You create a calligraphic border.

4. **Try creating a flower by setting the angle to 45, 90, –45, and then 180 degrees, stroking twice, and using an imaginary center around which you click (don't drag) the petals.**

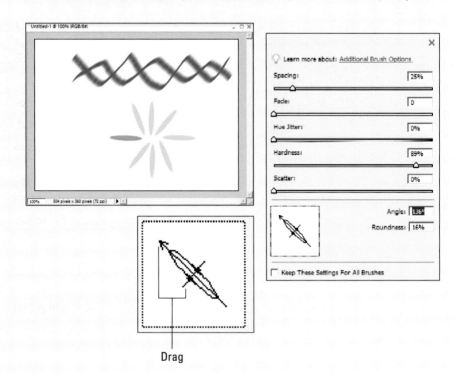

Drag

Saving your brushes

It's a shame to build a brush and not save it. Here's how to build your arsenal of brushes to save you time and effort:

1. **Right-click over the image.**

2. **On the Brushes palette, click the triangle and choose Save Brush from the flyout menu.**

3. **Name the tip and then click OK.**

   Make your custom brush name something you can remember. Scattering and other brush properties don't show up on the palette (although a fairly easy-to-see thumbnail image does appear in the Options bar preview box).

   After you click OK in the Save box, Elements wants to know the name of the current palette of tips.

4. **Name your new palette containing the custom brush tip something like `MyBrushes.abr`.**

   The unique palette name keeps you from overwriting existing brush collections.

Creating lines

Elements has a Line Shapes tool although it doesn't create rounded caps on lines. However, I know a way to create lines that doesn't require simplifying a shape before editing it — you drag while holding the Shift key, as follows:

✦ If you want a perfect horizontal or vertical line, follow these steps:

1. *Choose your Brush tool tip, size, opacity, hardness, and other attributes.*

2. *Click the tool on the image window and then Shift+drag (either left to right or up and down).*

   If your dragging is off by a degree or two, don't fret — Elements snaps your drawn line to the nearest horizontal or vertical axis.

✦ If you need a line drawn to something other than a 90° angle, follow these steps:

1. *Click a point.*

2. *Hold Shift and then click a finish point.*

Figure 3-8 shows the angular origami work you can quickly get into.

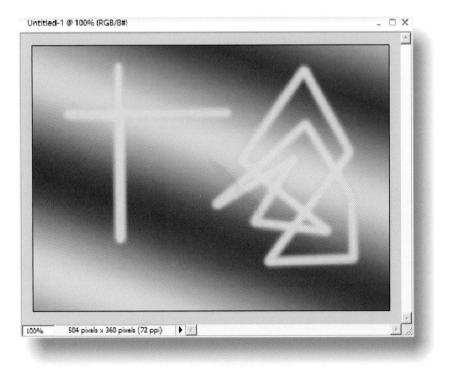

Figure 3-8: If someone asks where the line starts, hold Shift and point to the back.

Creating your own brush tip

To create your own brush tip, start at the Edit menu: Choose Define Brush (tip) from Selection. (Simply use Define Brush when the proposed tip is on a clear image layer.)

The Define Brush command isn't really useful unless you create a tip first. Brushes in Elements come in two kinds:

✦ **Tips created by math formulas:** These tips appear at the top of the Default palette, and all the More Options choices (such as Jitter and Spacing) are available for tweaking. You can't create a math formula brush from scratch; you can only set custom values in More Options for existing math formula brushes.

✦ **Tips created by sampling a selected bitmap area:** The tips at the bottom of the Default palette are bitmaps. You can't change the hardness of a sampled bitmap brush tip although all the More Options choices can be tuned.

Transparency can be built into a sampled brush tip by designing a tip on a transparent layer. (Layers are covered throughout Book V, and I squeak in some info here.)

My idea of a fun custom tip is a drawing of a water droplet. Follow along by opening my `Droplet.psd` file.

If you're in the mood, you can design your own tip so that you can sample it. Here are some guidelines for the brush tip design:

1. **Ctrl+double-click the workspace.**

2. **In the New dialog box, type** 65 **in both the Width and Height fields and then choose Background:Transparent.**

   A brush larger than 65 pixels isn't very useful although you can adjust its size up or down (from the Options bar) before you use it.

3. **Double-click the Hand tool to zoom your view way into your composition.**

4. **Use a very small, soft brush tip, like 3 pixels on the top Brushes palette row.**

5. **Paint a shape with black.**

   A sampled tip is grayscale with transparency — colors aren't figured in.

   You can vary the opacity of the tip in two ways:

   • Use shades of gray.

   • Paint with black and lower the Opacity on the Options bar. This is how I created the Droplet tip.

Putting It Together

Creating a Water Droplet Brush

Here's an example you can follow to create a water droplet brush:

1. Choose Edit⇨Define Brush from the main menu, name it in the dialog box, and then click OK.

2. Choose the tip from the palette (on the bottom row); then, in More Options, set Size, Scattering, and Spacing.

continued

continued

3. **Save the brush.**

   In the figure here, you can see that I painted water drops on a window pane (in a stylized way) using only about four strokes.

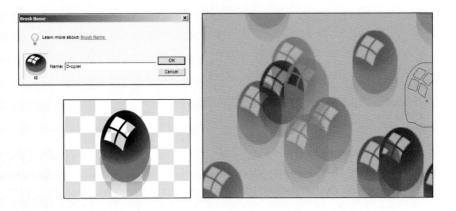

Painting a pattern to save

If you're diligent or if you own Painter, you can create a pattern brush:

1. **Create a *wrap-around design* (one that seamlessly tiles) on a transparent layer.**

   Defining and saving wrap-around patterns is covered in Book VI, Chapter 3.

2. **Define the design as a brush.**

3. **Set the Spacing to 100%.**

If you want to try using a pattern brush tip, follow these steps:

1. **Load the `PatternBrush.psd` file.**

2. **Set Spacing to 100%.**

3. **Shift+drag in rows from left to right (as shown in Figure 3-9).**

The Pencil tool

The Elements Pencil tool produces paintings whose color edges are extremely harsh; if you zoom into your Pencil work, you can see individual color pixels.

I can't think of a single use for this tool except to correct a single pixel in an image by using a 1 pixel diameter brush.

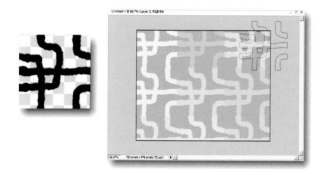

Figure 3-9: You can resize a pattern brush, but you can't do this with an Elements pattern.

When you choose the Pencil tool, all the tips on the palette are hard, too, but this tool has an interesting Auto Erase option as a check box on the Options bar. You stroke to lay down foreground color; then, when you paint over areas you've already colored, these areas switch to the current background color. Auto-erase happens on image layers as well.

If you want to really erase Pencil marks and not replace your strokes with the background color, use the Eraser tool. Figure 3-10 shows you my Pencil tool handiwork.

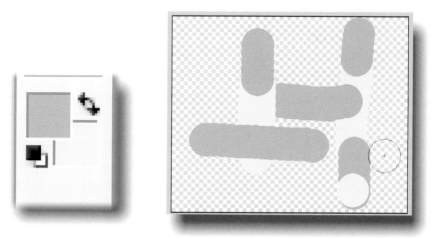

Figure 3-10: The Pencil tool is on par with the Microsoft Paint tools.

The Color Replacement tool

Use the Color Replacement tool to tint color or grayscale images to new and exciting colors. It replaces only the *hue* (the predominant quality of a color) and doesn't mess with brightness values.

The best images to colorize by using this tool have lots of medium grays but no pure whites or blacks. (You can't colorize pure black or white.)

The options for this tool don't affect your work much.

 Putting It Together

Turning Yellow Flowers Blue

Use the `Daffodils.png` image along with the following steps to replace the natural colors in the image:

1. **Choose the Color Replacement tool and then choose a medium pale blue as your foreground swatch.**

2. **Stroke over the yellow daffodils.**

3. **Stroke over the white areas.**

   You don't see any change, as I mention earlier in this chapter.

4. **Stroke over the green stems.**

   Lighter areas turn blue, and darker areas show little or no change.

The Color Replacement effect, as you can see in the figure here, can be used to create a black-and-white effect. You can also create a sepia (antiqued) tone in a photo by using brown. Or, create a vision of hell by using a red foreground color on an image (maybe like the one-horse hometown you left).

The Color Replacement tool is really the Brush tool in Color Blending mode, which you can see on the Options bar. Read more about blending modes in Book V, Chapter 3.

The Impressionist Brush tool

The Impressionist Brush samples photo colors in order to do its thing; clear areas on a layer receive white. The Impressionist Brush is a piece of fancy software programming, and you might have little call to use it in either serious design work or image retouching. For example

✦ The Impressionist Brush turns a nice photograph into something resembling an unwanted scalp condition by using any of ten Options bar presets.

✦ You can fine-tune the scalp condition by using different tips.

Impressionist Brush results look very little like work from Monet, Renoir, or Cézanne — and after all, Degas' impressionist paintings were quite realistic. For my money, there should be an adage that applying a preset filter to a photo doesn't produce art.

In Figure 3-11, you can see the Impressionist Brush applied to the daffodils photo from earlier in this chapter.

Figure 3-11: Elements isn't an instant art factory.

Flood-filling with the Paint Bucket

Use the Paint Bucket tool to flood a selection area with either flat color or a pattern, specify the degree to which the tool fills existing image areas, perform anti-aliasing, and do other tasks:

✦ Adjust the Tolerance option on the Options bar.

   • 0: Produces no effect

   • 255: Fills the entire image

✦ Select either Contiguous (only touching pixels are filled) or non-contiguous (every instance of the color you click over is filled).

✦ Anti-aliasing smoothes the edges between unfilled areas and areas you fill.

✦ Perhaps the neatest option is Opacity. On image layers, you click over an image area; the result is that a new color fills the image and the level of opacity you specify from the Options bar decreases the opacity of the fill on an image layer.

✦ The Pattern mode can be used to apply an Elements preset or your own pattern instead of flat color.

Putting It Together

Filling Color Areas

Here's an example of working with the Paint Bucket. To follow along, open
`Daffodils.png`.

1. **With the Paint Bucket chosen, choose purple as the foreground color.**

2. **Choose a Tolerance of 85 on the Options bar and then clear the Contiguous check box.**

Now when you click over the white of the daffodils, every daffodil white area is filled.

3. **Click over a daffodil, press Ctrl+Z, reduce the Tolerance to 15, and click again.**

In the figure here, you can see the difference that Tolerance settings make.

Filling a photo with flat color doesn't produce very interesting results, but try out the Pattern option with the daffodils.

High tolerance   Low tolerance

Putting It Together

Pattern-Filling Areas

I created a special pattern for the following steps to show how to apply a seamless pattern by using the Paint Bucket. Load `RedDaffodilPattern.psd` and follow along.

1. **Choose Edit⇨Define Pattern, accept the default name, and press Enter.**

2. **Choose Edit⇨Revert for the daffodil image.**

You want to restore the messed-up image without having to reload it.

3. **Choose the Paint Bucket, choose Pattern from the Options bar, scroll down, and then choose the saved pattern you defined in Step 1 from the Pattern drop-down palette.**

4. **With Tolerance at 85 and the Contiguous check box clear, click any yellow in the image.**

You should get results at least as strange as those shown in the figure here.

The Gradient tool

The Gradient tool is a must-have item in Elements. With it, you can

✦ Create a linear fade from the background color to the foreground color.

✦ Fill an area with a circular gradient, a diamond-shaped gradient, or a custom-designed gradient to feature multiple colors and opacities.

To use the Gradient tool, drag from one image area to a different position. The angle of your drag determines the

✦ **Angle of the resulting gradient (except with Circular)**

The position of the gradient start point is determined by your cursor's position when you start dragging.

✦ **Midpoint of the gradient, which often contains intermediate colors and can be wide or narrowing, all depending on the distance you drag**

Here are some visual examples of the different two-color transitions that you can create, as shown in Figure 3-12.

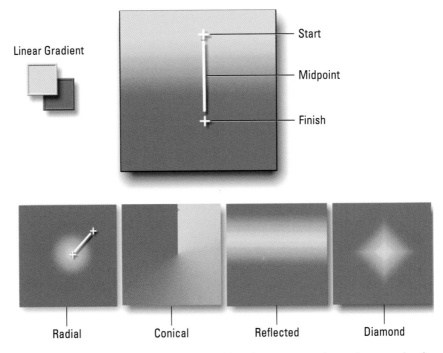

Linear Gradient

Start

Midpoint

Finish

Radial   Conical   Reflected   Diamond

Figure 3-12: The Gradient tool creates transitions between your chosen foreground and background colors.

You can choose from the Elements collections of preset gradients or design your own. Here's how to build your own gradient:

1. **Press D to set the colors as the ones you use as the "primer coat" for your custom gradient:**

- Foreground color (black)
- Background color (white)

2. **Choose the Gradient tool and then click the Edit button on the Options bar.**

   The Gradient Editor opens.

3. **Click the color stop — the checkered square with a triangle on its top — at the far bottom left of the black-to-white gradient ribbon.**

   The top stops are transparency stops, not color stops — don't mess with them.

   The Color box at the lower left is activated. See Figure 3-13.

4. **Click the Color swatch (which takes you to the Color Picker), choose a deep gray (this color plays a part in the more complex gradient you're building), and then press Enter.**

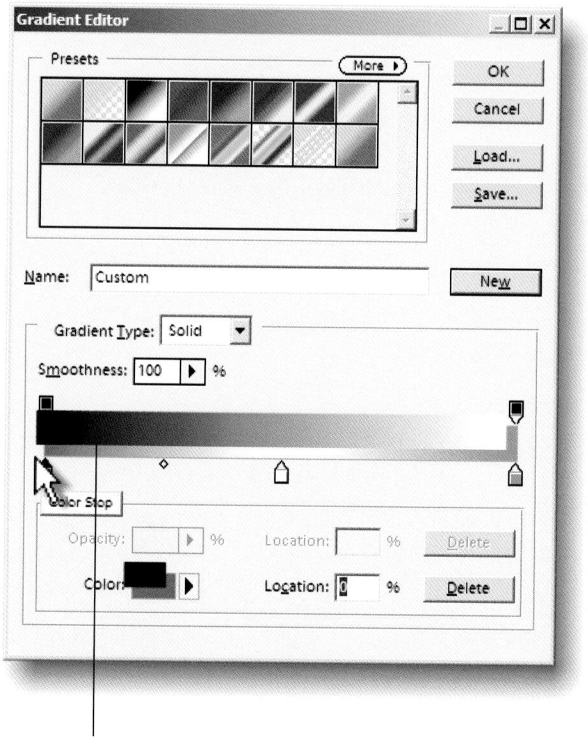

Color stop

Figure 3-13: The Gradient Editor is your ticket to building gradients of your own.

5. **Click just below the gradient strip in the middle of the strip.**

   This step creates a new color stop of the same color you defined for the far-left color stop. See Figure 3-14.

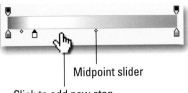

Midpoint slider

Click to add new stop.

Figure 3-14: Creating a new color stop.

6. **Drag the new stop to the middle of the color strip.**

7. **Click the Color swatch and then choose white from the Color Picker.**

8. **Click the right color stop, click the Color swatch, and then choose medium gray.**

   By adding stops and specifying different colors, you create a simple, multicolor gradient that's nice for image background replacements.

9. **Click a new stop and then drag it down.**

   This step deletes the stop from the gradient, just so you know how to remove color stops.

10. **Drag one of the diamonds between color stops.**

    This step sets the midpoint between color stops.

11. **Click just above the top of the strip.**

    A transparency stop is created, at the default 0% opacity. See Figure 3-15.

Transparency

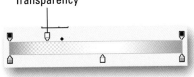

Figure 3-15: Creating a transparency stop.

   You set the opacity for transparency stops by using the Opacity number field. (Click the triangle to the right of the number field to access the much more convenient slider.) Drag the transparency stop away from the gradient strip to delete it.

12. **Click Save, name the gradient, save the whole collection in the following dialog box, and then press Enter.**

13. **Choose Noise from the Gradient Type drop-down menu and then choose HSB from the Color Model drop-down menu. See Figure 3-16.**

    The sliders affect how broad or narrow of a spectrum of color component goes into Noise — a frantic, happy, complex mode.

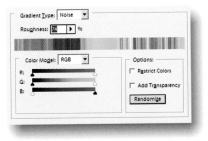

Figure 3-16: Choosing a gradient type.

14. **Drag the S(aturation) right slider all the way to the left and then drag the B(rightness) left slider a tinch to the right.**

You have a handsome, brushed aluminum gradient. Save it and admire your work.

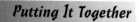

Putting It Together

Creating a Circular Gradient

An example of my favorites is a hand-cobbled, circular gradient. It's also a terrific gradient for archery lessons, supermarket sale signs, and ice cream trucks, as shown in the figure here.

Here's how to make a cartoon-style gradient by using the Gradient Editor:

1. **Set about four stops of red on the gradient strip. (Alt+drag to copy your first one to three other positions.)**

   Read about color stops earlier in this chapter.

2. **Make four yellow color stops between the red ones.**

3. **Drag the yellow color stops so that they overlap the red ones, to create abrupt, not smooth, color transitions, as shown in the figure here.**

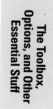

continued

continued

4. **Find a picture. A lighthearted image —
   a simple doodle or a photo of one of
   your friends — in TIFF or JPEG format
   works well.**

   I chose a favorite cartoon character.

5. **If you want to add text, read Book VII
   on using the Type tools.**

6. **Use Circular mode, accessed from
   the Options bar, to drag this gradient
   from the center away to the image
   window edge.**

   See the results in the figure here. Try Conical
   mode for awesome sunburst effects.

The Cookie Cutter tool

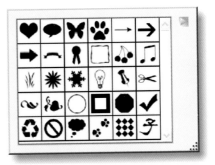

Beneath the Crop tool (see Book IV, Chapter 1) is the Cookie Cutter tool, which
is a hybrid of the Magic Eraser and the Shapes tools (covered in Book IX,
Chapter 4).

You use the Crop tool on background images — images without special
layers — to instantly convert them to Elements layers and erase the outside
areas. Here's how:

1. **Choose a shape from the collections accessed from the
   Options bar.**

   In this example, I chose a heart
   shape. Use any shape you like; just
   right-click with the Cookie Cutter
   over the image window to display
   the default palette. Additional
   palettes can be loaded from the
   palette's flyout menu (click the triangle icon). See Figure 3-17.

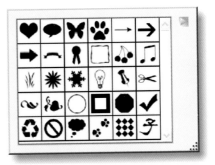

Figure 3-17: Choose any shape you want
from the Cookie Cutter palette.

2. **Drag the shape over an image
   area and adjust its width or
   height position by dragging a corner of the bounding box.**

   You can rotate a Cookie Cutter selection, too. Just hover your cursor
   over a bounding box corner until you get a two-headed bent arrow
   cursor, and then drag up or down on the corner.

3. Reposition it by dragging in the center and then press Enter.

The layer contents outside the shape are erased, as shown in Figure 3-18.

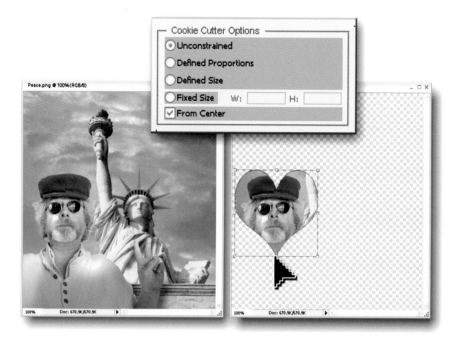

Figure 3-18: The Cookie Cutter is a perfect, one-step means to creating scrapbook items.

Background images — images without special layers — are instantly converted to Elements layers, and the outside areas are erased.

Cookie Cutter Options, on the Options bar, enables you to make a Cookie Cutter selection starting at the center rather than edge to edge.

The Type tools

The Type tools are used to add to an image anything from a simple headline to paragraph text. They are straightforward to use, very much like the tools in a word processor.

The Type tools are so important that they're explained throughout Book VII.

The Red Eye and Straighten tools

The Red Eye and Straighten tools are covered in Book VI, Chapter 1.

The View tools (Zoom and Hand)

The Zoom and Hand tools are intuitive to use if you're even a little experienced with graphics programs, but I don't assume that, so here's the skinny on both.

The Zoom and Hand tools don't work when you're free-transforming a selection or when you're working with a plug-in or other dialog box. The window scroll tabs can't be used, either, but the Ctrl++ (plus) and Ctrl+– (minus) keys can.

The Zoom tool

The Zoom tool enables you to zoom into an image window in two different ways:

+ **Steps:** Click in the window to zoom to whatever magnification you desire: 200% or 300%, for example. You can't change these predefined percentage steps.

  You can press Ctrl++ (the plus key) without choosing the Zoom tool.

+ **Stepless:** Elements also offers stepless zooming — zooming to any percentage, not just whole, even numbers.

  You can zoom into 341% or 595% viewing resolution, for example, by marquee-dragging the Zoom tool.

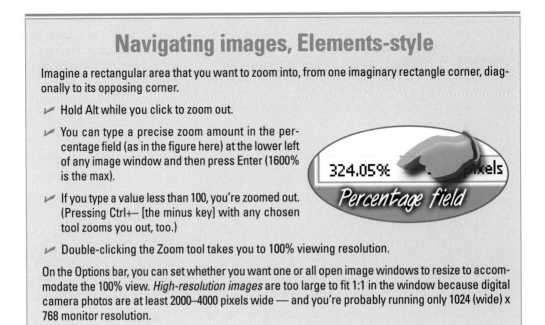

Navigating images, Elements-style

Imagine a rectangular area that you want to zoom into, from one imaginary rectangle corner, diagonally to its opposing corner.

✏ Hold Alt while you click to zoom out.

✏ You can type a precise zoom amount in the percentage field (as in the figure here) at the lower left of any image window and then press Enter (1600% is the max).

✏ If you type a value less than 100, you're zoomed out. (Pressing Ctrl+– [the minus key] with any chosen tool zooms you out, too.)

✏ Double-clicking the Zoom tool takes you to 100% viewing resolution.

On the Options bar, you can set whether you want one or all open image windows to resize to accommodate the 100% view. *High-resolution images* are too large to fit 1:1 in the window because digital camera photos are at least 2000–4000 pixels wide — and you're probably running only 1024 (wide) x 768 monitor resolution.

The Hand tool

The Hand tool is used to pan an image window that contains an image that's larger than its window. Here are your options and shortcuts:

✦ Double-click the Hand tool to zoom out so that the entire image can be seen onscreen.

✦ Hold the spacebar to toggle to the Hand tool from any tool.

Additionally, you can use some keyboard shortcuts for scrolling your view of images that are too large to see in whole at 1:1 viewing resolution, and they work when any tool is chosen:

✦ Use the Home key to move a zoomed-in view to the upper-left corner.

✦ The End key moves your view to bottom right.

✦ The PageUp and PageDown keys can be used to scroll the image window.

The Healing Brush tools

The Healing Brush tools are covered in Book VI, Chapter 2.

The Eraser tools

The Eraser tools are documented in later chapters through hands-on projects.

✦ **Eraser:** This tool erases to the background color on the Toolbox when you're erasing on an image *Background* and erases to transparency on a layer.

✦ **Background Eraser:** This tool doesn't work, and Adobe is aware of it.

✦ **Magic Eraser:** This is a one-click deal. Click over an image area (on the *Background* or on a layer). Based on image color similarity, it removes to transparency either

• Similar-color pixels that touch each other (Contiguous)

• All instances of similar colors (the Contiguous check box cleared on the Options bar)

You have the following options when you use the Magic Eraser:

• **Anti-alias:** A smoothing option on the Options bar.

• **Tolerance:** Sets how similar colors need to be to be erased; 255 is the maximum, in which every pixel in the image is deleted.

• **Sample All Layers:** Samples the range of colors from all layers although only the current layer gets this color range erased. It's a novel, but not awfully useful, feature.

The Shape tool

The Shape tool is covered in Book IX, Chapter 4.

The Focus tools

The Focus tools, as shown in Figure 3-19, are used to apply sharpening or blurring to only a part of an image.

To sharpen or blur an entire image, use the Blur and Sharpen filters.

Suppose you download a Windows Metafile (.wmf) as a bitmap from the Microsoft site. It will have jagged edges because few metafile converters anti-alias WMF files. The remedy is to use the Blur tool. You simply stroke over the edges of the design to create intermediate color steps, to smooth and blur the design edges slightly. The Blur tool creates transition colors along a harsh edge between a design's foreground and background. In Figure 3-20, you can see how this jaggy WMF can be enhanced.

Figure 3-19: The Focus tools.

+ **Blur:** The Blur tool can be used effectively to remove or reduce skin flaws in portrait photography.

+ **Sharpen:** The Sharpen tool increases contrast between pixels where you stroke.

Figure 3-20: The Blur tool creates transition colors along a harsh edge.

The Sharpen tool can create nasty blotches in image areas. If you need to sharpen an image area, I suggest that you select the area, feather it, and then choose Filter➪Sharpen➪UnSharp Mask.

+ **Smudge:** The Smudge tool smears pixels a little less precisely than the Filter➪Distort➪Liquify filter, and can be used with great results in hiding and eliminating dust and other minor image flaws. See Book VI, Chapter 1.

The Toning tools

Use Toning tools — Dodge, Burn, and Sponge — to adjust the brightness values in the area you stroke over.

Toning tools don't affect the hue of an image.

Both burning and dodging change the saturation in an image area; the Sponge tool is used after dodging or burning but can be used on its own to reduce *color clipping* — areas so saturated in inkjet prints that sometimes ink puddles result. Unfortunately, reducing clipping using the Sponge tool is a trial-and-error deal. You have to pull a bum print first to see where you need to desaturate to then make a good print.

The Dodge tool

The Dodge tool can brighten highlights, midtones, or shadows in an image.

The best use of the Dodge tool is to highlight image areas to add sparkle — say, to a photo of a metal object or to highlights on ocean water to perk it up.

In Figure 3-21, I "polished" a dull object by using the Dodge tool, to bring out interest and depth.

Brightening midtones and shadows decreases image contrast. You'll be unhappy with the results.

Figure 3-21: Polishing an area with the Dodge tool brings out compositional dimension.

The Burn tool

The Burn tool does the opposite of the Dodge tool — it deepens areas. You want to burn shadow areas (not midtones or highlights).

The overcast golf course image shown in Figure 3-22 becomes deeper and prettier when I burn the trees (sorry, Smokey).

Figure 3-22: Burning weak shadow areas reinforces them.

The Sponge tool is also a good special effects tool. In Figure 3-23, I wanted to remove the color in the image background so that viewers home in on the pretty girl. By using Desaturate mode of the Sponge tool, I don't need to carefully select the girl or background and use Hue/Saturation to remove the background color. (Selection work is necessary with most image editing, and it's tedious.)

You might be happier with the results by selecting problem image areas and then using the Levels command (Ctrl+L) to correct tone deficiencies.

Figure 3-23: You need to reduce, more than add, saturation in most images.

Exploring the Options Bar

The Elements Options bar is your key to unlocking the full power of the Toolbox.

Before you use a tool, make it a practice to check the Options bar to see whether the options for a tool are really the ones you need. The Options bar remembers previous settings, and this memory can muck up your work. The Options bar is *contextual* (changes to show options for a specific tool).

Using the Contextual Menu

Think of the contextual menu as the Windows Properties menu:

1. You right-click an interface element, such as an image window, to bring up options or functions, such as layer choice, when the Move tool is chosen, or blend modes when the Paint Bucket tool is active.

2. The contextual menu (like the Options bar) changes menu items to reflect the possibilities of the tool you're using.

The contextual menu replaces some (but not all) of the need for the Options bar. Some tools have no options. Selection tools, though, can be modified by right-clicking in the selection, and painting tool size can be adjusted by right-clicking to display the Brushes palette.

Using the Photo Bin

The Photo Bin can't be detached from the interface, but it can be hidden by clicking the icon labeled in Figure 3-24. Unlike in other Windows applications, when a file window is minimized, an Elements image doesn't fold down to the title bar. Instead, the image goes to the Photo Bin, where you can see a big thumbnail of it. You restore images by clicking their thumbnails, which provides a convenient way to work with multiple files.

Figure 3-24: The Photo Bin is where you restore all images loaded in Elements.

Photo Bin is more than just a gallery. You can perform minor image edits and get image info in a jiffy:

+ Right-click a thumbnail to quickly rotate an image.

+ Right-click a thumbnail to duplicate an image.

✦ Add File Info to an image by choosing this option via the right-click contextual menu. This method is quicker than choosing File➪File Info, and
it's a convenient way to copyright and add other information to several
images (see Chapter 2 of this mini-book).

Using Image Windows

Two things aren't obvious when you open an image file:

✦ **The image background**

Beyond the edge of a photo in a window is the *image background,* which
isn't part of your photo. Rather, it's a space that when revealed, enables
you to use selection tools clear to the edge of a photo. You drag the image
window border away from the photo to reveal the gray background.

You might need to zoom out to see the entire photo.

✦ **The Document Sizes field**

The Document Sizes field appears to the bottom left on the image window
horizontal scrollbar. By default, this field tells you the image's file size as
it's saved to disk. Then, you can see after the backslash how large the
file is during editing. The right-side amount changes as you add layers
and save selections. If you click the arrow, you can display other information, as follows:

✦ **Document Profile:** Tells you what color space, sRGB or Adobe RGB, the
photo occupies. This info is *static* — it doesn't change — so this setting
isn't helpful to keep displayed.

✦ **Document Dimensions:** Tells you the dimensions and the *resolution*
(how many pixels per inch of the active image), which is very useful.
To set this readout to inches, pixels, or another increment:

1. Press Ctrl+Shift+R to display rulers.

2. Right-click a ruler.

3. Choose the increment.

4. Hide the rulers.

✦ **Scratch Sizes:** Shows you how much temp space is set up for Elements
(determined in Preferences, Ctrl+K) and how much is presently used.

If the used amount is approaching the allotted scratch disk size, you
have problems, and Elements never alerts you about it. If your scratch
disk value is bordering on critical, try one of these methods:

- Choose Edit⇨Clear⇨Undo History after you save your edited file.

- If clearing history doesn't do the trick, close Elements and restart Windows. (It's better than getting an application halt error, which trashes your work, forces you to restart your machine, and possibly changes your political views.)

✦ **Efficiency:** Tells you how much memory is being used. If Efficiency drops below 50%, take these necessary measures:

- Save all your work (take your time and get your editing the way you want it) and then choose Edit⇨Clear⇨All.

- If this doesn't restore your Efficiency, press Ctrl+Q and restart Windows.

Consider buying a utility package, such as the Iolo System Mechanic ($50; www.iolo.com), which can defrag and retrieve memory (RAM) on the fly without restarting Windows. Windows, since 1995, is supposed to retrieve memory reserved by applications that hang on to memory even after they're closed (indicating a poorly written program), but this is folklore.

✦ **Timing:** Tells you how long an editing process or filter took to run. (This info is fairly useless.)

✦ **Current Tool:** Redundant because the tool you're using can be seen on the Options bar.

I recommend that you set Document Sizes to Efficiency; you can click directly on the field to get image dimensions. See Figure 3-25.

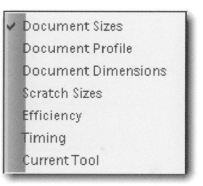

Figure 3-25: The Document Sizes field.

Setting Image and Canvas Size

A photo's *dimensions* — the width and height and number of pixels per inch — are displayed on the bottom lip of the image window to the right or in the zoom field. Another way to determine and change photo dimensions is to right-click the image's title bar. In the Image Size dialog box (see Figure 3-26), you can set the image size. If you select Resample Image, you change the image data and make the photo smaller or larger.

Don't resample an image upward. The result stinks.

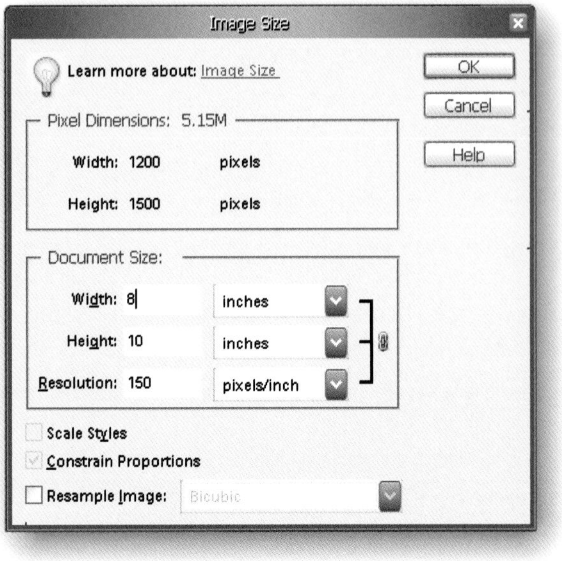

Figure 3-26: Change photo dimensions here.

When you reduce a photo, make sure to specify Bicubic Sharper to keep the image crisp. If you disable Resampling, the image data doesn't change because you're decreasing or increasing physical dimensions only by decreasing or increasing (printing) resolution. Say you have a 4" x 5" image at 300 pixels per inch (ppi). The image is sort of small to print, so you increase the dimensions to 8" x 10", and Elements decreases the resolution to 150 ppi (which is fairly okay to make an inkjet print). Even though you haven't changed the pixel information in this case, Elements still asks you to save the image because the structure of the image data has changed.

Canvas Size can either

✦ **Increase the size of the image window:** Leaves border room to paint.

✦ **Decrease the size of the image window:** Crops the image but doesn't change the pixel colors remaining. Elements alerts you to cropping.

Click any of the "chiclets" in the Canvas Size dialog box (see Figure 3-27) to tell Elements in which direction you want additional canvas.

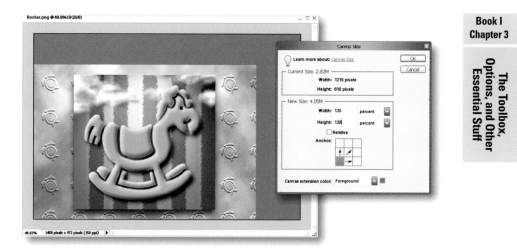

Figure 3-27: Change photo dimensions here.

Chapter 4: Palettes and Shapes

In This Chapter

☞ **Exploring palettes and their options**

☞ **Letting Elements do the work creating special effects**

☞ **Getting the lowdown on layers**

☞ **Using filters, styles, and effects**

☞ **Using shapes to create design elements**

*P*alettes are graphical menus, Adobe-style. Elements sports a *Palette Bin* as a means of quickly accessing a layer property, an effect, image information through palettes, and other essential tools and features. All palettes have a common scheme: You can minimize them by clicking the little triangle to the left of their title, and the More button displays options specific to the palette. It's here also that you can set the size of their thumbnail previews. Large is a good choice, especially if you're running a high screen resolution.

Shapes are vector designs (see Chapter 2 in this mini-book) that can be used as scrapbook items; Styles and Effects can be applied to shapes, and they can be scaled and rotated without losing their crisp edges. Elements ships with a huge collection of shapes, and you can add to this collection by downloading user contributions from

    http://share.studio.adobe.com/
        axBrowseSubmit.asp?t=14

You can't create shapes of your own by using Elements, but if you have a friend who owns Photoshop, they can create shapes for you, so remain their friend.

Cruising the Elements Palettes

By default, in the Palette Bin, you can find the How To, the Layers, and the Styles and Effects palettes. But more palettes — palettes that you need — are under the Window menu. Here's what my investigating turned up.

The How To palette

The How To palette is always there for you. Like other palettes, you can drag its title bar off the Palette Bin to float the palette in the workspace, but if you then close it, it returns to the Palette Bin. How Tos include detailed instructions on performing a lot of common Elements tasks, such as how to create an old-fashioned photo. The How To palette is interactive; you can either read the description of a step, or the palette will do the step for you. See Figure 4-1.

Figure 4-1: Let the How To palette guide you step by step.

Don't mistake the How To palette for Elements' Help system (Help⇨ Photoshop Elements Help, or press F1). You actually have three resources for Elements assistance if you count Help⇨Tutorials (four, if you include this book).

The Layers palette

Layers are an integral part of Elements image editing; Book V covers working with layers in detail, but for now, I just deal with the operation of the palette.

By default, when you open an image, a Background (layer) thumbnail is displayed. When you open an image taken with a digital camera or work from a different bitmap design program, many of the Layers palette's options aren't available. This is remedied by double-clicking the Background thumbnail, which opens a dialog box in which you can name the layer (a good practice to get into, especially when working with a multiple layer image). In Figure 4-2, you can see the Layers palette with callouts indicating the basic options; most of them are self-explanatory. I cover Adjustment layers in Book V.

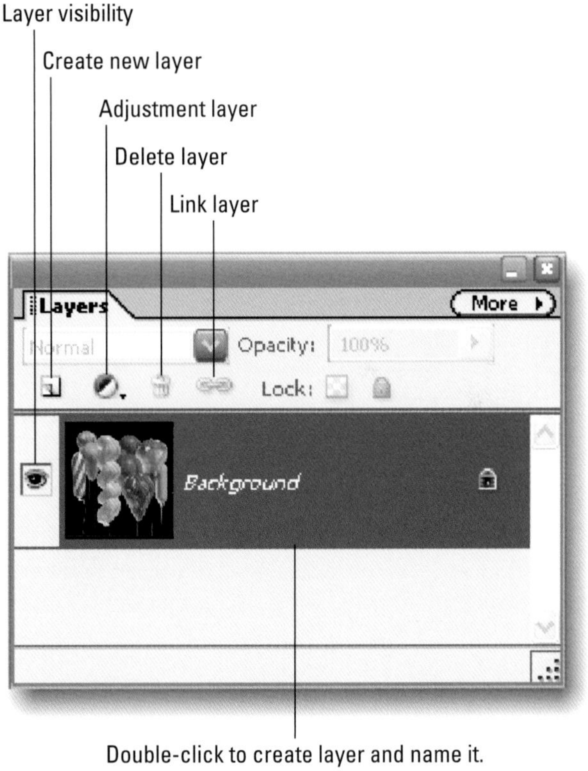

Layer visibility

Create new layer

Adjustment layer

Delete layer

Link layer

Double-click to create layer and name it.

Figure 4-2: Many controls for image layers are found on the Layers palette.

The Link Layer option enables you to move the contents of two or more layers:

+ To link layers, Shift-click the layer thumbnails you want to link (like the two images in Figure 4-3), then use the Move tool on your linked layers.

+ To unlink layers, click a single layer thumbnail.

Lock everything.

Transparency | Layers are linked.

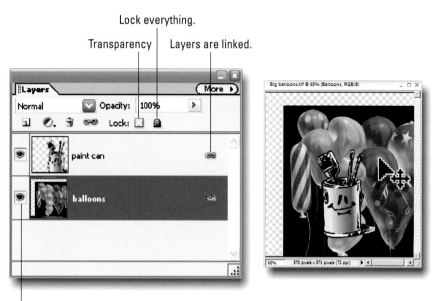

Hide/Show layer

Figure 4-3: Layers can be linked and locked.

You cannot link the opacity or blending modes between layers.

A layer can have its transparent regions *locked:* You can't paint into these areas with this option checked. (You can lock transparency, layer content position, and blending mode when you click the Lock All padlock-shaped icon.)

The eye icon to the left of a layer title is the show/hide button. You click it to make the layer invisible (and not editable) in the image window. You restore visibility by clicking the area to reveal the eye icon.

The Styles and Effects Palette

Styles, Effects, and most of the plug-ins under the Filter menu are accessed from this palette. You double-click an icon or drag the icon into an image window. More than one style can be added to an image layer: A style can be disabled, simplified, or removed by right-clicking the *f* icon on a styled layer and then choosing an option.

More options for a styled layer can be found by double-clicking the *f,* as shown in Figure 4-4.

Figure 4-4: Find stylized options here.

Filters

Although you can choose Filter⇨Filter Gallery to peruse the special effects filters (there are other filters than those offered in Elements; you'll see how to display and use them in later chapters), dragging a palette icon into the image window just takes you to the Filter Gallery in most cases. Filters, such as Shear, pop up a simple dialog box when you choose them.

To use the Filter portion of the Styles and Effects palette:

1. **Choose Filters from the drop-down list.**

2. **Choose from a subcategory, such as Artistic. Thus, you don't have to scroll forever to find a filter you want.**

3. **Drag the icon from the palette into the image window (alternatively, you can double-click the desired filter icon), and poof! You get the Filter Gallery interface.**

In Figure 4-5, I chose the Water Color filter, and after choosing options for the filter, you can see the result.

Resize the Filter Gallery and scoot it out of the way a little so you can compare your original image in the workspace with the preview of the effect.

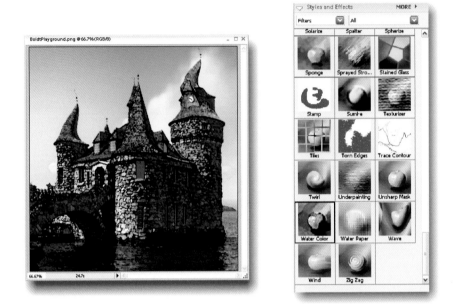

Figure 4-5: Applying a filter is a matter of dragging and dropping an icon.

You'll get less stylized and more eye-pleasing results with the Water Color, Dry Brush, and many other filters if you choose the *smallest* brush size, the *most* detail, and — where offered — the *least* texture.

Effects

Elements Effects are *macros* — a list of editing moves and filters that run automatically at a speed you can't discern.

Effects can be used to create textures, anything from slime to a brick wall. Choose Filters from the drop-down list on the palette and then drag the icon into a new image window. Effects are created on layers that the Effects macro builds by itself, and you can use several Effects on successive layers within one image file. See Figure 4-6.

Styles

Styles can be applied to an entire image layer or to a shape that you create within the image. You can apply a style on top of a shape that already has a style, too. Styles are varied — you have at your cursor tip everything from glows to drop shadows to bevels and even more complex Styles.

Bricks   Green slime

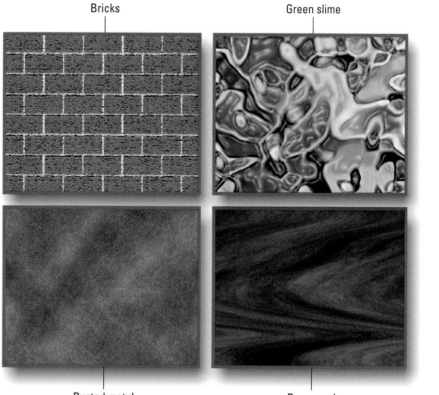

Rusted metal   Rosewood

Figure 4-6: Effects are easy to generate.

 Putting It Together

Applying Styles

Follow along with these steps for an example of applying the Cactus style:

1. **Ctrl+double-click the workspace to create a new document.**

   Choose Transparent as the Background contents and then press Enter.

   Styles layers work only on layers.

2. **With the Lasso tool (press L), drag any sort of shape that you like.**

 continued

continued

3. **Press Alt+Backspace to fill the shape.**

   The shape is filled with foreground color. **Note:** Any foreground color is okay because the style you use comes with its own shading. However, a style needs pixels (the foreground color in this case) on a layer in order to work.

4. **Press Ctrl+D to deselect the marquee selection you created in step 2.**

5. **Choose Styles from the Styles and Effects palette drop-down list and then choose Complex as the subcategory.**

6. **Drag the Cactus thumbnail on top of your doodle.**

   Instant art!

7. **To add a bevel to the art; choose the Bevels subcategory and then drag any thumbnail into the window. I used Chrome Fat.**

   See the results in the accompanying figure.

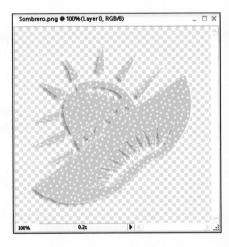

Features found in other palettes

The Styles and Effects palette might be the coolest palette in Elements, but the other palettes are invaluable for undoing mistakes, setting selection area colors, and other editing and enhancing work.

Undo History palette

Elements lets you go back in your work to undo mistakes, and the Undo History palette is your road map. Press F10 (or choose Window➪Undo History) and take a look at how you can save yourself from pressing Ctrl+Z all the time.

Try some time-travel practice navigating History with these steps:

1. **Open an image.**

2. **Double-click the Background title on the Layers palette to convert it to a layered image.**

3. **Select an area by using any of the selection tools and then cut the selection to a layer (right-click and choose Layer via Cut from the contextual menu).**

4. **Delete the bottommost layer by dragging its thumbnail on the Layers palette onto the Trash icon.**

   You have four editing moves listed on the Undo History palette. You can move to that editing point in time or drag the slider (to the left of the titles) up or down.

Group the Undo History palette with the Layers palette; see Chapter 3 in this minibook for instructions. Alternatively, you can put the Undo History palette in the Palette Bin (you can make space by closing the How To palette after you've exhausted its info); just click the More button and then click Place in Palette Bin When Closed.

Color palette

There's no keyboard shortcut to the Color palette, so you might want to open it from the Window menu and park it in the Palette Bin — or group it with a palette you use frequently. To specify a color from the palette, click the swatch; that color loads as the Toolbox's Foreground color swatch.

The Color palette is customizable:

✦ You can quickly choose colors you've used before (which is indispensable when you're retouching skin tones or need to match colors for product photography).

✦ You can use Photoshop (for Windows) color palettes in Elements. Find a willing friend who owns Photoshop (for Windows) and then copy the collection to Elements' Presets↪Color Swatches folder when Elements is not running.

To set colors, follow these steps:

1. **Choose the Eyedropper tool from the Toolbox and click over a color area in the image.**

2. **If you want to add a sampled color (it now appears as the Foreground color swatch at the bottom of the Toolbox) to the current color collection, hover your cursor over a blank area of the color collection on the Color palette and then click.**

   The Color Swatch Name dialog box appears, and you can now name the color. See Figure 4-7.

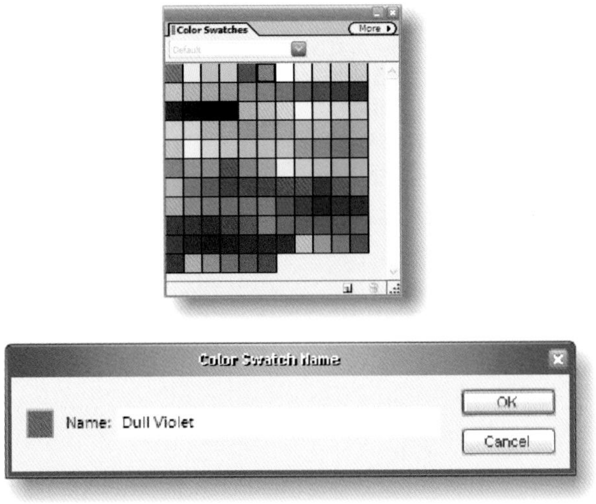

Figure 4-7: Save your new colors or they won't be on the palette if you switch color collections in the future.

Accessing color collections

Elements ships with several Color palettes. To choose a collection, click the drop-down list on the palette.

✦ **Save sampled colors to the existing collection by choosing Save Swatches from the More flyout menu.** Choose a new name so you don't overwrite an existing collection. (Or use `Blank.aco`, a palette I built that has only one color, available at the *For Dummies* site where you download the example images.)

✦ **If you want to delete a color from a collection, hold Alt and click over the color swatch.**

✦ **Click the More button and choose Small List. You have other display options on the flyout menu, but this my favorite display.**

Histogram palette (F9)

The Histogram palette tells you whether an image needs a trip through the Levels command (Ctrl+L).

A *histogram* isn't a painful surgical process. It's actually a display of an image's brightness properties in a graph style.

In Elements, pixels are evaluated in different ways; one evaluation method is by the number of pixels that have highlight brightness, or midtones, or make up the shadowy regions of an image. The Histogram palette shows you the population of pixels possessing these three ranges of brightnesses (also called *value, lightness,* and *tone*) in the whole image or within a selection.

In Figure 4-8, I selected just the face in the picture, the most visually interesting part of the image. And the selection's contents appear to be well balanced from a tone standpoint. It has few shadows as well as plenty of midtones, and the midtones gradually fall into highlights. Use your own eyes first and then use the Histogram palette to confirm your evaluation of an image's exposure in various regions.

The midtone range in photos typically contains the most visual information.

Navigator palette (F12)

The Navigator is a palette that lets you scroll the image window when your zoom level makes the image larger than the workspace.

In a typical editing session in Elements, you have enough palettes eating up valuable screen space without one more. When you use the Zoom and the Hand tools, you don't need the Navigator palette.

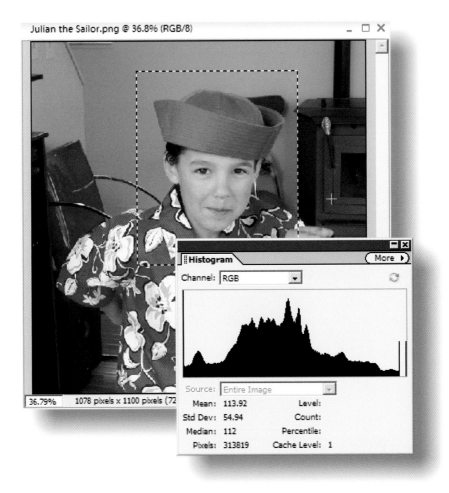

Figure 4-8: Use your eye to judge a photo's tone balance and then use the Histogram palette.

If you're not comfortable with the Zoom and Hand tools, here's how the Navigator palette operates:

1. **You first need an image to navigate. Load an image that's larger than can be displayed onscreen at 100% viewing size.**

2. **To navigate the image, follow these steps:**

   - Drag the Navigator's slider left or right to scale your view of the image.

   - Drag the red outline in the Navigator preview to move to an area of the image you want to view onscreen (an area that is outside of your view).

   Figure 4-9 shows the Navigator palette used to pan my view of a 4000 x 3000 pixel photo.

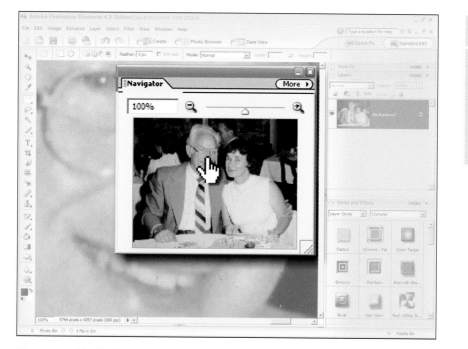

Figure 4-9: The Navigator is fairly fast to use, but so are the Zoom and Hand tools.

Info palette (F8)

This palette helps you discern the color of any image area over which you hover your cursor in a variety of color specifications, such as HSV and Grayscale. You are also provided with the coordinates of your cursor position within the image (x is width; y is height) and how large of a selection you might have made.

Follow along to obtain — and tinker with — information about an image:

1. **Open an image.**

2. **With the Rectangle Marquee tool, drag a selection.**

3. **Look at the bottom-right field on the Info palette.**

   By default, it displays the height and width of the selection in pixels, as shown in Figure 4-10.

	X :	709
+	Y :	726

Figure 4-10: Find image info here.

4. **Change pixels to inches.**

   a. *Click-drag the crosshairs on the bottom-left Info palette field.*

   b. *From the drop-down menu, choose Inches.*

5. **Click the eyedropper icon on the upper right of the palette and then choose Grayscale.**

   Now, wherever you hover your cursor in an image, you'll be told both the RGB value under your cursor and simultaneously how bright the underlying area is. Figure 4-11 shows customized Info values for the current image.

Figure 4-11: The Info palette is a great addition to grouped palettes.

Palette options

All palettes have options, which are
accessed by clicking the palette's More
button. Some palettes have more useful
options than others, namely because
options pertain mostly to features of the
Palette controls. The Brush tools actually have a palette; it's docked on the
Options bar, but you can call up the
Brushes palette when a painting tool is
chosen by right-clicking in an image
window. And this palette has a More
button.

Perhaps the most useful option —
thumbnail display — is on the Layers
palette. Click More and then choose
Palette Options. With all of us using
high screen resolutions these days, a
large layer thumbnail can help you to
see the contents of a layer, as shown in
Figure 4-12.

Figure 4-12: Palettes offer more info and
options when you click More.

Using Shapes and the Shape Tool

Unlike any other object creation tool, the Shape tool makes *vectors* — invisible
paths that you or an Effect fills. Vectors have two advantages over pixel-based
designs:

- ✦ Vectors can be scaled and rescaled without loss of detail. Pixel designs
  lose quality when resized.

- ✦ Vectors retain edge crispness, while pixel designs get fuzzy when
  transformed.

Shapes occupy their own layers, a new layer is created for every new shape
you create, and the exterior of a shape on its layer is transparent. However,
you can't apply a gradient to a shape until you click the Simplify button
(or right-click a Shape thumbnail on the Layers palette and do the same).

You can make a fairly sophisticated composition by using only shapes.
There are plenty of options for shapes, and the Custom Shapes collection is
positively vast. Shapes include a rectangle and oval, but you can easily use
the rectangular and elliptical Marquee tools to make these shapes and fill
them without the Simplify step. There's a rounded rectangle Shape tool, as

shown in Figure 4-13; you have options in the same place as the other Shape tools, in the area under the triangle you click on the Options bar. And in the number field, Radius, you can enter a pixel dimension — 20px, for example — to create rounded corners. A high value results in a circle, so stick to values of 60 pixels or less.

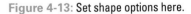

Figure 4-13: Set shape options here.

Shapes are filled with the current color on the Options bar. If you want two shapes on different layers to have different colors, you first create the Shape and then choose its color (or style).

The Line Shape has options for adding arrowheads to the head or tail of lines. You set the Concavity on the Option bar's flyout menu to adjust the pointiness of the arrowhead tail; adjust Width and Length to set the overall shape of the arrowhead. If you use a value less than 100%, you get a signpost effect and not an arrow jutting out of the line. Line Shapes, unlike the rectangles, can be drawn at any angle (in any direction), which makes it a terrific tool for annotating directions over an image of a road map. See Figure 4-14.

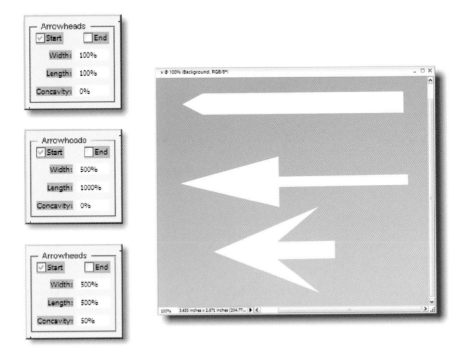

Figure 4-14: Basic shapes are useful for directions and for placed text.

The Move tool doesn't create shapes. Instead, use it to reposition, rotate, and scale a shape. The Move tool can move shapes around on their layers, and you can free-transform a shape by pressing Ctrl+T and then dragging a corner bounding box handle. To apply any transformation, press Enter.

The thin black outline around shapes doesn't print but does go away when you simplify a Shape layer. I believe this is just program code left over when Adobe engineers ported Elements from Photoshop CS2, where shapes — called *paths* — can be manipulated by their outline.

The Polygon Shape has two basic options — regular and star — which you access by clicking the down-pointing icon to the right of the speech balloon icon (the Custom Shape tool). This flyout menu is where you control whether you make a star or polygon as well as whether the points are sharp or soft. You control the number of points from the Sides field on the Options bar. In Figure 4-15, you can see the Polygon tool at work; in a later Putting It Together section, I explain how to make this hollow star shape by using the Subtract mode.

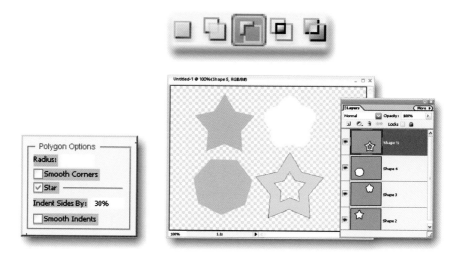

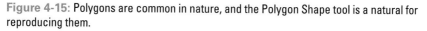

Figure 4-15: Polygons are common in nature, and the Polygon Shape tool is a natural for reproducing them.

The Custom Shapes tool is packed with just about every conceivable ornament and doodad you can imagine. Right-click in an image window to display its palette and then click the flyout arrow to choose a collection palette.

Catch a falling star (and other shapes)

To add to your Shapes collection, you can

- **Ask a friend who owns Photoshop to build you a palette.**

  You cannot create Shape presets in Elements.

- **Surf to** `http://share.studio.adobe.com/axBrowseSubmit.asp? p=2`, **where fellow Photoshoppists post free Shape palettes.**

  Copy the files to your *Your Drive*`\Elements 4\Presets\Custom Shapes` folder while Elements isn't running.

With all Shape tools, you *constrain proportions* — keep the shape undistorted — by choosing this option from the Options bar's flyout palette, accessed by clicking the little down-pointing triangle. This is inconsistent with the behavior of the rectangular and elliptical selection tools, so don't try holding Shift when creating shapes.

Putting It Together

Using the Styles and Effects Palette with the Custom Shape Tool

Here's how to create a beautiful piece of art, without painting, but using the Styles and Effects palette in combination with the Custom Shape tool. You'll be surprised at how simple Elements makes it to don your artist's *chapeau* and amaze your friends.

1. **Ctrl+double-click the workspace to call up the New dialog box.**

2. **Choose Default Photoshop Elements Size; then press Enter.**

3. **Choose Effects from the Styles and Effects palette; then open the Textures category.**

4. **Double-click the Bricks icon (or drag the icon into the image window).**

5. **Choose the Elliptical Shape tool, click the down-pointing triangle on the Options bar, and then choose Defined Proportions.**

   This keeps the circle circular and not oval.

6. **Drag a circle in the image window; color doesn't matter in this experiment.**

   This figure shows the black circle shape on a layer above the brick style.

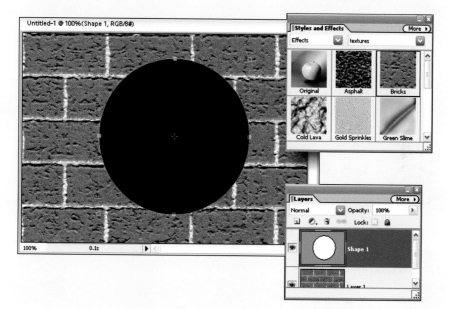

7. **Click the Custom Shape tool on the Options bar.**

8. **Choose the Ornaments collection and then click the fleur de lis icon.**

9. **Click the Subtract mode icon (the third icon of the joined rectangles) and then drag a fleur de lis anywhere, a little smaller than the circle.**

   In Subtract mode, no new shape layer is created.

10. **With the Shape Selection tool (top left on the Options bar), drag the fleur de lis so that it's inside the circle.**

    See the following figure. On your own, try the Add and Intersect mode to make extremely complex shapes.

continued

continued

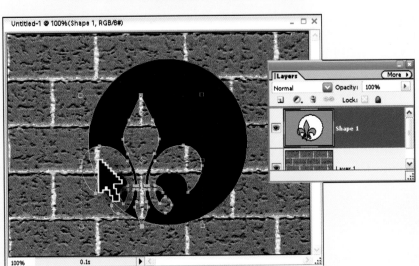

REMEMBER

If you want a Shape to be transparent with the rest of the layer filled, click the Selection tool, click the Shape, and then click the Subtraction mode button.

11. From the Styles and Effects palette, choose Layer Styles and then the Wow-Plastic collection.

12. Drag the Wow-Plastic Aqua Blue icon into the window.

Notice that the button is semitransparent: You can see the bricks underneath in this figure.

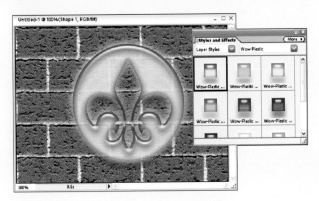

13. **Add a drop shadow by choosing the Drop Shadows category, and then drag a shadow icon into the image window.**

Layer styles can be stacked on the same layer, as shown in the figure here.

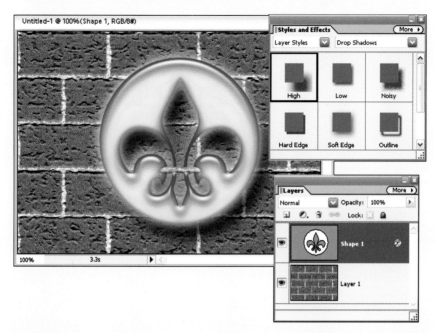

The tiny *f* next to a layer title on the Layers palette displays controls for the effect. Double-click it to get to Style Settings. The bad news is that if you apply two different styles to a single object layer, you can't separate one style from another by using Style Settings. If you want more control over styles for more personal artwork, follow these steps:

1. **Apply a style.**

2. **Set your settings, such as Bevel Size for Wow-Plastic.**

3. **Simplify the layer.**

4. **Apply another style and then use Settings to fine-tune the new style.**

Book II
Acquiring Images

The 5th Wave   By Rich Tennant

"Mary-Jo, come here quick! Look at this special effect I learned with the new Elements software!"

*E*verything has an origin. Plants come from seeds, kittens come from cats, mountains of work come from your boss or client, and even images have to come from somewhere. In this mini-book, you become acquainted with ways to get images and artwork into your computer and into Elements. Digital cameras, photo CDs made from 35mm film, scanning photos, and different graphics programs can all help you acquire your images. Book II lays out all the details about procuring images.

Chapter 1: Input from a Digital Camera

*W*orldwide consumer digital camera sales reached nearly 53 million in 2004 and are estimated to reach 82 million units in 2008. Already, worldwide unit sales of consumer digital cameras surpassed worldwide unit sales of film cameras.

If you don't own a digital camera yet, you're missing out on a wonderful opportunity. Digital cameras and Elements go together like politics and cronyism.

You can find the example file that I use at the end of this chapter at www.dummies.com/go/ PhotoshopElementsAIOFD1e.

Make: NIKON
Model: E880
Date Time: :00-04:00
utter Speed: 1/60
F-Stop: f/7.8
Ratings: 100

Digital Cameras 101

If you're thinking of retiring your analog film camera, digital cameras require almost zero retraining time — you can get right down to business snapping away and importing your labors to Elements after no more than a half-hour spent reading the owner's manual. The following sections address the future and present owner — what make and models you can choose, image resolution capability, and other considerations.

Camera types

Digital cameras come in two different flavors: the SLR, which is basically a film SLR camera with the film area replaced with sensors; and the viewfinder, which is nothing like the el cheapo film camera your folks gave you when you were 11.

Digital cameras come from many of the same folks who make film cameras: Nikon, Canon, Olympus, Fuji, and Kodak all offer digital camera models to suit your needs and budget. Basically, the types of digital cameras are

✦ **SLR (single lens reflex):** An advantage of an SLR is that you look through the lens to frame your subject and to focus. You can also change lenses. SLRs are more expensive than rangefinders.

Figure 1-1 shows two digital cameras.

Figure 1-1: SLRs and rangefinder digital cameras fit the budgets of professionals and hobbyists alike.

✦ **Rangefinder (point-and-shoot):** Rangefinders cost about half as much as SLRs. However, you can take excellent photos with them, and many offer telephoto zoom and macro options for close-ups. You don't look through a little pop-up frame anymore, though. Most rangefinder backs are an LCD panel (see Figure 1-2) whose size varies from model to model — some screens are the size of a large postage stamp, and others are as large as half a playing card.

Many digital cameras can also take movies, and newer models can also capture sound. However, these movie clips are necessarily short because memory cards (more about those later in this chapter) can hold only so much information at the rate of 15 frames per second (fps). Although it's nice to add movie clips to Elements creations, movie frames are small — typically 352 x 240 pixels. However, I recommend that you use your digital camera to take movies, particularly if the occasion is special. Then, choose File⇨Import⇨Frame from Video to do serious image editing or to print a frame.

Figure 1-2: Most rangefinders feature an LCD panel on back.

Camera capabilities and formats

Camera resolution is measured in *megapixels* (millions of pixels). In 2006, the 6-megapixel (MP) camera is common; that's 5,947,392 pixels per frame. 6MP translates to a 2816 x 2112 pixel image.

In non-nerd terms, an uncropped 6MP image is 8 ¼" x 11" photo at 256 pixels per inch (ppi), which exceeds inkjet printer resolution and is more suitable for a fine-photography coffee table book.

Digital cameras can also take lower-resolution images, but you can mix and match sizes on a single memory card in a single session. The number of photos that you can take and store on a single memory card varies depending upon the size of the image and also the compression you use, which has to do with file format.

The three common photo file types are TIFF, JPEG, and Raw (or DNG). Camera compression is a choice you have when you decide upon the file format for saved images — a decision you make before shooting. Raw files are compressed without data loss; JPEG images comprise image data where some original data is discarded at the time you shoot the image. TIFF, on the other hand, is an uncompressed data type — every pixel you capture is preserved.

If you're capturing a very important event, go with TIFF or Raw.

TIFF: Uncompressed

The TIFF file format, as written by digital cameras, is a clean image, like Raw but without compression.

Uncompressed TIFF at 6MP will fill a 128MB memory card with about seven exposures, which is an unacceptable number for weddings, graduations, and other events.

JPEG: Lossy compressed

JPEG, even though it's lossy compression, produces acceptable images at a 10:1 compression ratio. (A 1MB JPEG expands to 10MB when opened.) And you can get a lot of pictures on your memory card.

JPEG images can have some nasty stuff going on because of their compression:

+ **Noise:** Even on a robin's egg blue day, you'll see some *noise* (random distribution of different color pixels) if you zoom in close. (Usually, the noise isn't visible on inkjet prints.)

+ **Color casting:** If you zoom into some trees, you'll see magenta or other color casting. JPEG wasn't meant to handle sharp color transitions from area to area.

  This color casting usually won't print — shifting to dark brown or black — because inkjet printers have a small color space. For more info on color spaces, see Book I, Chapter 2.

Weaknesses in JPEG technology vanish when you resize an image down for an e-mail attachment. Figure 1-3 shows the random distribution of different colored pixels (noise) and color casting that the JPEG file format produces, even though the image colors are pure and the image focus is sharp.

Raw (DNG): Losslessly compressed

The Raw image file format is your best bet for precious images because it offers 10:1 lossless compression.

This is a relatively new format. A digital camera you bought three years ago might not save to Raw.

Working with Raw images in Elements is a little different than working with TIFFs and PSDs. I cover all your options later in this chapter.

Getting images into Elements

Downloading your images from a camera to your hard drive is painless, thanks to Adobe Systems. My suggestion: Use a memory card reader to download digital images from your camera instead of the umbilical USB cable that comes with the camera. Those nifty tethers drain a camera's batteries severely.

Noise in sky

Magenta cast in tree edges

Figure 1-3: JPEG isn't the best format for serious photography.

Time to get some terminology out of the way. Here's the lowdown on memory cards and card readers:

✦ **Memory card:** This is the "film" for digital cameras. Memory cards come in different varieties, each one proprietary to a specific brand of camera. The predominant memory card types are the CompactFlash and the Memory Stick; see Figure 1-4. SanDisk is the one of the biggest vendors of memory cards, with Hitachi, Olympus, PNY, and other distributors out there. Buying a name brand you're familiar with won't necessarily get you a better card because most cards are made by a small number of plants and are licensed for distribution only by large, recognizable companies. Typically, you can get a 512MB memory card for $70 or less, but the memory market is extremely volatile — prices change, usually in a downward direction, from day to day.

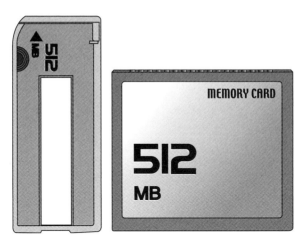

Figure 1-4: Memory cards are proprietary.

Like being prepared with extra rolls of film, you should have two or more memory cards so you can swap cards when you've filled one.

✦ **Card reader:** You plug this device (see Figure 1-5) into your PC and then you pop in your memory card (preceding bullet) in the reader to download images. Usually, a card reader comes with your camera; if it didn't, you can buy one for $40–$50. Again, name brands don't assure name-brand quality. Epson, SanDisk, Toshiba, Adaptec, and others distribute card readers under their own name. Before you buy a card reader, make sure that it reads the form factor of the memory you have; many readers are multiformat, but check before you buy.

Figure 1-5: Use a card reader to download images.

A Web cam — those tiny guys you can pick up at a drugstore for $10 — is not a serious imaging tool, nor is it intended to produce photos of a quality and resolution that you can edit or print from Elements. Web cams are intended to download via an umbilical cord directly to the Web for posting.

Downloading digital images

Downloading images is a snap. (Sorry; very bad pun.) Here's how:

1. **After you have your card reader hooked up and you insert a memory card, Windows pops up a Device Detected options box.**

2. **Click the Organize and Edit Using Adobe Photoshop Elements icon, as shown in Figure 1-6.**

   Don't select the Always Do the Selected Action check box because you might have an iPod or a music CD plugged into your computer.

3. **Click OK.**

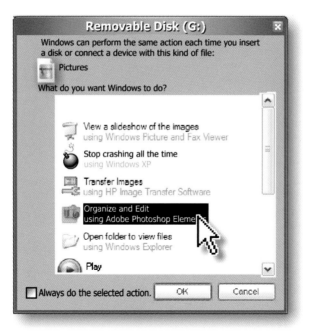

Figure 1-6: Choose Organize and Edit from this dialog box.

Here's where the fun starts and Elements Organizer (see Figure 1-7) starts up. *Organizer* is a module within the Elements suite that helps you create your favorite collections of photos (it's not the Editor module). Read Book I, Chapter 1 if you're not familiar with Organizer.

Figure 1-7: Create collections here.

1. **Tell Organizer from what device you want to load images by choosing your card reader from the Get Photos From drop-down list (top right of Figure 1-8).**

2. **Choose a folder on your hard drive for the download.**

At this point, you can have Organizer fix any red-eye problems with your photos (which I cover later in this chapter): Just enable the Automatically Fix Red Eyes check box. However, auto red-eye reduction is not foolproof:

- Elements has little way of discerning Willie from a Winnebago in a photo.

- You will wait while Organizer ponders and processes.

Figure 1-8: Use Organizer to down load digital images.

You're presented with all your images in a nice, big thumbnail-style.

3. Choose the images that look good and suit your needs.

- With your cursor in the thumbnail field, press Ctrl+A to select all.

    or

- Mark the check box to the right of specific images to download 'em. Refer to Figure 1-8.

4. Click the Get Photos button after you check off your faves.

Organizer puts your images in the catalog, which you then tag for your collection(s).

Organizer won't download images already in the catalog from a previous download to the same location on your hard drive. And it politely tells you which files will not be downloaded, as shown in Figure 1-9. See Book I, Chapter 1 for information on the Organizer module and creating collections.

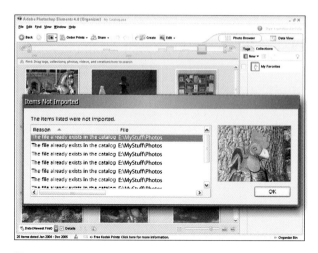

Figure 1-9: You can't write a file from a camera to the same hard disk location twice.

I can't think of any reason why you'd want to save the same image twice, though. Organizer is merely stopping you from accidentally overwriting newer (probably edited) files with older ones.

5. **Click OK and then go get a ham sandwich and some lemonade.**

   Your next screen is merely a download progress report, as shown in Figure 1-10. Watching a progress bar is as entertaining as watching paint dry.

Figure 1-10: Well, at least it tells you the destination folder if you forgot.

Clearing your memory card — or NOT

When Organizer finishes downloading photos, it asks whether you want to *clear the card* — that is, delete the images from the card.

When you see this warning, click No emphatically. (See Figure 1-11.) Every camera formats memory cards differently; if you allow Elements to *reformat* your card (an efficient way of deleting everything), there is an excellent chance your camera won't be able to read or write to the card.

Figure 1-11: Do not allow Elements to delete files from a memory card.

To clear a card, do one of the following:

✦ Delete unwanted photos manually from the card after it's back in your camera.

✦ Use your camera's formatting capability to wipe the card.

Setting post-download options

After you download your photos, you're still not quite set to edit your images. You'll want to decide whether to keep embedded printer info in your images as well as whether to keep version sets.

Bypassing embedded printing information

Many cameras embed inkjet printer information into a digital image, so printing without editing first is a possibility.

In Figure 1-12, you can see an attention box that Elements pops up, saying the inkjet info will go kaflooey if you edit this image. "So what?!," I retort, and you should, too, by clicking OK.

Figure 1-12: Go ahead and dismiss this alert.

Saving as a version set

If you choose to let Organizer fix red-eye as part of the download process (see the earlier section, "Downloading digital images"), you'll wait a little while before Organizer tells you and shows you which images have been corrected. Elements does this corrective work on a copy of the image and saves the corrected image to a version set. (See Figure 1-13.)

Figure 1-13: If Organizer auto-corrects red-eye, the original file won't display in Organizer.

When Elements repairs an image — or if you open an image in Elements Editor from Organizer — you have the option to Save As in a version set. You then view only the most currently edited image in Organizer; the original is safely tucked away on your hard drive, and your edited image has the file-name you chose, appended with an `_edited-1`, `_edited-2`, and so on.

The only disadvantage to saving as a version set is that you can open the older original only by loading it manually and not via Organizer — Organizer won't show the different versions in the catalog window.

Exploring the Raw Mini-Editor

Raw images cause Elements Editor to load a special interface; some, but not all Elements features are available, but you can save a copy of a Raw file and then edit away on the copy.

What is Raw?

A Raw file is often referred to as a *digital negative,* also known as a `myfile.dng` file (although you see the image onscreen and not a film negative or anything like that). Different camera manufacturers use different file extensions for Raw formatted files; for example, Canon cameras write `*.crw` files. Don't drown in the details, though, because Elements handles the idiocy of confusing extensions; Adobe covers just about every digital negative format out there.

Nikon, Konica Minolta, Olympus, Canon, Sony, Fuji, Kodak, Pentax, and other camera manufacturers offer Raw as an image saving option. Read the specs on the camera you intend to buy, and make certain it saves to Raw. Also, because there are different Raw standards, choose from the manufacturers I list here to ensure that your camera's Raw files are compatible with Elements. Adobe has done a wondrous feat in creating Raw import filters for 99 percent of the cameras out there, but you don't want to own a camera that writes to that other 1 percent. I suggest you avoid digital camera brands such as Uncle Fred's PixelCam.

There are a number of advantages to shooting Raw:

✦ **Compactness:** A Raw file uses lossless compression and is typically one-tenth the size of an equivalent TIFF image.

✦ **Processing:** No processing is done by the camera, such as sharpening or white balance. This gives you — and Elements — total control at editing time.

✦ **Saving:** Raw images can be saved to 16 bits per color channel, which I explain later in this chapter.

Exploring a Raw image in Elements

If you have a Raw format image handy, load it into Elements. If you don't have a Raw file, you can download my `David.dng` file. The first thing you'll notice, besides the interface, is that your camera model, the digital film speed (the ISO), aperture, and shutter speed are all on the title bar. Nice! This info is recorded in *metadata* (a text header added to image files that can be read as text when the image is open) fields in File⇨File Info, too. (And it doesn't go away if you crop or use Save As.)

This sample file is a 2MB DNG file.

On the Adjust tab (see Figure 1-14), you have color temperature settings. Usually, Elements can get the temperature from the camera info, but you can choose user-friendly settings such as Fluorescent or Daylight from the White Balance drop-down list. The histogram tells you how much of each of the red, green, and blue color channels contribute to the makeup of the photo. So, for example, if you see too much blue cast in the histogram, adjust the Temperature and Tint sliders to fix it. The histogram changes to reflect the new color cast.

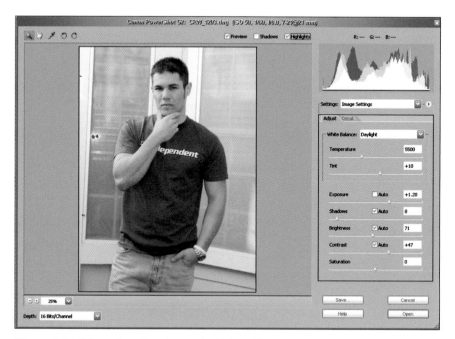

Figure 1-14: Take and use Raw images for high quality.

Your other options beyond color correction on Raw files are to show color clipping and to save to 8 bits per color channel, or 16 bits. *Color clipping* is the display of color areas that are *out of gamut,* beyond the viewable or printable range. Enable the Preview check box and the Shadows check box to preview black point clipping; enable the Preview check box and the Highlights check box to preview white point clipping.

+ **Black point clipping:** From an inkjet printer, a black point clipped area prints a muddy puddle of color in shadow areas. Your options to solve black point clipping are

    • Decrease the saturation on the whole image. (Suggestion: Don't.)

    • Remember this area (take a screen capture of the image with clipping showing, for accurate reference), convert a copy to 8-bit mode in Elements, and then use the Sponge tool in Desaturate mode on problem areas.

I hope that Elements version 5 will show color clipping on 8-bit images in the Editor.

+ **White point clipping:** Fortunately, white point clipping requires no adjustment for color printing because these whiter-than-white areas won't be rendered — the white of the paper simply shows through. Refer to Figure 1-14 to see an image in the Elements Raw editor.

The Daylight balance seems like a good setting (mostly because it's an outdoor photo), and there's no black point clipping and a little white point clipping.

If you have a Raw file, save it to 16 bit, which I explain in the following section.

Elements Editor has no color clipping previews — you must shoot in Raw format and use the Raw editor to see clipped areas.

Book II
Chapter 1

Input from a
Digital Camera

8 bits of data in a 16-bit bucket

Here's an analogy that supports working with 16-bit images until you need other Elements tools: Suppose 16-bit mode is a gallon container into which your camera pours three quarts of pixels. Whenever you use sharpening, color casting tools, or the Levels command, Elements remaps original color pixels — in effect, compressing the image data — and sort of losing some pixel values, sloshing over the sides of the container. After editing, you might have only two quarts of pixels remaining in the container. Now, perform the same tone and color adjustments on an 8-bit copy of the same image — say there's a quart of pixels in this 8-bit (call it a quart) container. You lose some pixel values as the image is compressed. When the 16-bit image is converted to 8-bit mode (Image➪Mode➪8-Bits per Channel), your quart container is topped off with pixel values, but the 8-bit (quart) image contains less than a quart. Working with "what you can't see" results in a net loss that's superior to working on an 8-bit copy. And you can see the difference.

Moving to a higher color level

Images have red, green, and blue components, or *channels*.

✦ An 8 bit per channel image is the image type you use most in Elements. An 8 bits per color channel means that an image is 24 bit and is capable of featuring up to 16.7 million unique colors.

✦ A 16 bit per channel image, such as Raw, is called a *48-bit image,* capable of expressing 281 trillion unique colors, several more than I can count on my hands.

However, logic becomes murky when dealing with 48-bit images. Computer video *subsystems* — the video card and monitor — handle 24 bits of color information and no more. Apparently, working with image data you can't see is like the guy on the subway who converses with Martians about the helium crisis in America. Expensive color print presses (not an inkjet printer) can handle 48-bit images and will produce images of noticeably better quality than 24-bit photos can, so think about spending a little money on an art print for a competition. Second, although many of Elements' features such as Layers, paint tools, and Shapes can't be used in 16-bit mode, you have Levels (Ctrl+L), Hue/Saturation (Ctrl+U), and cropping tools at your disposal.

Figure 1-15: Work between 16-bit and 8-bit modes to preserve and enhance details.

Don't worry about this image editing compression stuff because many images need data to be discarded to focus on the important details of an image. I did a little color correcting while the image (of Figure 1-14) was in 16-bit mode. (The photo was pretty outstanding right out of the camera.) In Figure 1-15, I converted a copy of the photo to 8 bits per color channel (decreasing the file size to 50 percent of the original, from 22MB to 11MB). Then I used the Straighten tool, cropped the image, performed a little masking work on the subject, blurred the unimportant background, and darkened the background a touch. The halo effect was deliberate — a New Wave touch. All this required some effort, but I got a better image than if I'd started with an 8-bit image. A similar effort is easily justified when you imagine that you're getting every penny's worth out of Elements and your camera.

See Book VI on image correction for techniques to restore and enhance 8-bit photos using the full complement of Elements tools, filters, and other features.

Chapter 2: Input from a CD

Y ou can find the example files for this chapter at www.dummies.com/ go/PhotoshopElementsAIOFD1e.

Kodak Picture and Photo CDs

If you haven't become a member of the digital camera revolution yet, there's still a few miles left on your film camera, and getting physical photos into your PC is very simple: You put them into your floppy drive (I'm *kidding!*). No, Kodak technology makes digital files from your film negatives a reality that won't bust your purse, and the quality and resolution of your film-to-digital pictures makes Kodak's PhotoCDs yet another way to edit your precious images to unparalled heights using Elements.

Getting CDs with Pictures

Even if you don't have a digital camera, you can still get — and thus edit — digital images. In a nutshell, you drop off a roll of traditional 35mm film at your photo-finisher (supermarkets and drug stores with film departments can handle your order), who sends it to the nearest place that rents and operates a PCD writer (a très expensive piece of hardware that reads film and writes the data to CD). In about three to five days, the film is developed, and you get your negatives and a Kodak Picture, Photo, or Photo Pro (for larger film sizes, such as 4" x 5") CD. Don't bother with 110 film; the negatives are too small to create a digital image of high enough resolution to work with in Elements or to print. Even if the operator took your 110 roll and didn't break out in peals of derisive laughter, your images would show film grain the size of golf balls.

Kodak to the rescue of Elements users

Kodak's Photo CD technology isn't new. It's been around for more than a decade, and it's still the best way to get your physical photos into your computer and Elements — with better quality than scanning images, which is ideal if you're not ready to buy a digital camera.

The Picture CD

Picture CD photos aren't a suitable size for serious image editing but are instead intended for e-mailing to your friends. For around nine bucks a roll, you get your negatives developed (prints are optional) in as little as one hour and also a Picture CD that contains 1024 x 1536 pixel (lossy compressed) JPEG images. Included on the Picture CD is a basic image editing utility — although I bet you never use it after you're experienced with Elements.

You don't need to order prints when you order a Photo CD. You can also ship other negatives to be digitized. Larger format negs (negatives) can be written to a special, more expensive Photo CD Pro Master Disc. Chromes (positives) are special order; the slides are removed from their mount for sampling but remounted again at an additional charge.

The advantages to Picture CDs are the price, speed of processing, and quality of the scans. Plus, a Kodak CD writer can scan film better than you can.

Negative-scanning devices that produce digital images will run you from $400–$500, and I've never been happy with my own Nikon model compared with Photo CD images. And those adaptors you can buy for — or that come with — your flatbed scanner are not only a pain to use but turn out crummy images. Dust is the biggest problem, next to a consistent, unwanted soft glow around image edges.

The Photo CD

Like the Picture CD, the Kodak Photo CD is made from high-resolution scans of your film but with several important differences.

A Photo CD is written to a proprietary file format, PCD, that few programs outside Photoshop and Elements can read. PCD files are *multiresolution,* which I explain in a moment. There's the actual photo scan, and then various different resolutions you import to Elements. A PCD file generates different image sizes on the fly.

There are only two quirks to Photo CD images:

✦ **Dust on the film can appear (mostly in sky areas) as white pinholes; see Figure 2-1.**

Evidently, it's not Kodak's responsibility to clean the film for scanning.

Pinholes

Figure 2-1: On a Photo CD image, dust on the film original can appear as pinholes.

✦ **PCD images were originally intended for viewing on your television.**
Kodak still has TV Photo CD players in its warehouse.

Analog television (not high definition HDTV) uses a different color space than your computer's monitor. As a result, Photo CD images appear bright and washed out in Elements until you correct them; see what I mean in Figure 2-2. Hopefully, Kodak will get the message soon that Photo CD technology has been adopted by photographers and not couch potatoes.

Uncorrected Photo CD image   Corrected in Elements

Figure 2-2: Photo CD images need a little love in Elements.

Before you order a Photo CD, here's a list of particulars and suggestions.

✦ **Rush, please:** Ask the photo place to put a rush on your order. It costs no extra; in fact, it just prompts the Photo CD technician to put your order at the top of the pile. Photo CD images go for anywhere between 80 cents to $3 for a special order Master Disc.

✦ **Thumbnails:** The jewel case of a Photo CD features image thumbnails. Although they're too small for reference, the thumbnails do give you a quick idea of a Photo CD's contents. Lose the jewel jacket, and you're in hot water because all Photo CDs look identical.

Photocopy the jacket and file it in a good place.

✦ **Identification:** Use a waterproof fine-point marker to write the volume name of the CD *on* the CD (for example, PCD2048), along with keywords.

✦ **Quantity:** In theory, a Photo CD can hold up to 150 exposures, or around six rolls of 24-exposure 35mm film. However, I've had only a single roll put on a Photo CD at a time because I was in a rush, and my Photo CD collection is needlessly large as a result.

Copy only the image files you really want to store on your hard drive, organize them, and rename them (which doesn't affect the data at all). Then burn a regular CD with as many PCD files as the CD can hold.

Using Photo CD images in Elements

Unlike TIFFs, PNGs, or JPEGs, Elements Organizer cannot add PCD format images to your catalog.

At the end of this chapter, I show you an option to organize PhotoCD thumbnails.

Here's how to load images from a Photo CD:

1. **Carefully put the Photo CD in your CDR-W drive or DVD drive.**

   Either type of drive works for PCDs.

2. **Double-click the workspace in Elements to open a file.**

3. **Choose the path in the Open box to**

   Your Drive:\PHOTO_CD\IMAGES

4. **Open the Images folder and choose an image.**

   Elements displays a thumbnail of the image in the Open box, as shown in Figure 2-3.

Figure 2-3: Elements shows you a thumbnail of the file you choose.

You can Shift-click to open multiple files, just like regular image files.

5. **Click Open.**

You're presented with a dialog box containing important options:

- **Pixel Size:** Choose the 1024 x 1536 version.

  By default, Elements wants a 64 x 96 pixel copy created.

- **Resolution:** This option sets a smaller dimension image at higher print quality as you choose larger resolutions. Choose 250 ppi for print, or 72 ppi for posting on the Web. You usually want to edit a large picture, so press Ctrl+Alt+I to scale a copy of the image down (use the Bicubic Sharper option) for Web display.

  This option doesn't affect the image size.

- **Color Space:** When you choose 16 bits per channel, you can work with extremely high-quality images, as I explain in Chapter 1 of this mini-book.

Figure 2-4 shows the Kodak PCD Format dialog box. Table 2-1 lists the file size options and what they're suitable for.

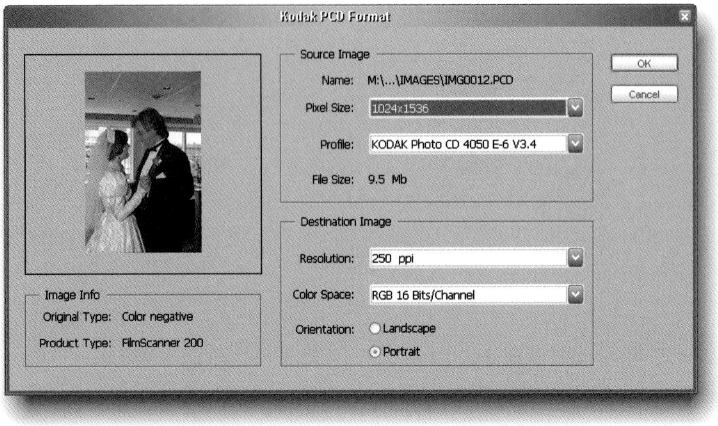

Figure 2-4: Choose file size and proportion here.

Table 2-1	Photo CD Image Sizes
Size	*Usage*
64 x 96 pixels	Ridiculously small thumbnail
128 x 192 pixels (Base/16)	Thumbnail
256 x 768 pixels (Base/4)	Suitable for TV
512 x 192 pixels (Base)	Okay for the Web (1.13MB)
1024 x 1536 pixels (4 Base)	Actual image (4.50MB)
2048 x 3072 pixels (16 Base)	Blown-up image (18.00MB)
4096 x 6144 pixels (64 Base)	Photo CD Pro Master Disc only

After the image loads, I suggest a quick trip to Quick Fix to adjust tone and possibly color. Photo CDs are balanced for television broadcast YCC color space (one channel of luminosity and two for color, a completely different color space from RGB); because you cannot adjust this when importing the image, use Quick Fix. In Figure 2-5, you can see the marked difference in the PCD image after just a click on the Smart Fix button in Elements Editor and then a click on Auto Levels in the General Fixes panel.

After correcting the Photo CD file's exposure, you've got a 16-bit (per channel — it's really a 48-bit image) image that you can tone and color correct manually in Elements Standard Edit mode and also crop. However, in 16 bits, most of the enhancing and paint tools don't work. To perform advanced editing, convert the image to 8 bits per channel — after correcting the exposure. As I discuss in Chapter 1, exposure correction when an image is 16 bits per channel comes out better, with less original information loss than correcting tones in an 8 bit per channel image.

Figure 2-5: Use Quick Fix to adjust tone and color for Photo CD images.

After preliminary correcting, follow these steps to perform editing that cannot be done in 16-bit mode:

1. **Choose Image⇨Mode⇨8-Bits/Channel.**

2. **Add layers; use the Clone Stamp tool and other advanced features.**

   Layers coverage is throughout Book V, and details on using the Clone Stamp tool can be found in Book VI, Chapter 2.

3. **Right-click the image title bar and choose Image Size.**

   You'll probably want to change image resolution to make the image fit in an 8" x 10" frame.

4. **In the Image Size dialog box (see Figure 2-6), clear the Resample Image check box.**

   Resampling changes the image data.

Figure 2-6: Change resolution here.

5. Type 7 in the Height field.

With a 1024 x 1536 PCD photo, decreasing image dimensions increases image resolution, and the new height (and width) will fit well when printed and put in an 8" × 10" frame.

As image dimensions shrink, image resolution increases; 174 pixels per inch resolution works well with most inkjet printers. Figure 2-7 shows a close-up of the Image Size box.

Figure 2-7: After cropping, increase the resolution by decreasing the photo's dimensions.

Kodak PCD technology enables 18MB files to be culled from the 4MB base image without blurring or other loss of image quality. So if you plan to crop an image *substantially,* do it on an 18-megger so you're left with a photo of sufficient resolution to print.

6. Save the file to hard disk (I recommend the PNG format).

Use a name that's both evocative and will point you to the Photo CD in the future.

For example, I named this wedding picture `Wedding Dance 2489 0021.png`, which I can later recall by the Photo CD volume and the image's user-unfriendly name. For reasons unknown, Elements wants to write the saved PNG file to your Photo CD, which is read-only, so stay alert as you wade through all those files!

Third-Party Cataloging

Elements won't catalog your Photo CD images, so your logical recourse is to search out a third-party application that'll do the job. I've found a very fast and inexpensive program that fits the bill, which I describe in the following section.

Getting around Organizer

Obviously, it would be nice if Organizer could catalog PCD files. It would also be nice to be young and rich. As a workaround, for $60 (the cost equivalent of dinner and a movie for two), you can get IMatch (`www.photools.com`), which is an extremely powerful, wizard-enabled image, video, and audio database program that indexes PCD images and (frankly) runs rings around Organizer. If you're dead-set on keeping your analog film camera, Photo CDs will be in your foreseeable future, and IMatch can manage the impossible. Unlike Organizer, IMatch uses a standard database format (Organizer is proprietary), so manipulating your image data in Excel, for example, is a snap. Like Organizer, IMatch can tag your files with description fields and IPTC (creator-protection parameters) data. (Read more about IPTC in Book I, Chapter 2.)

To use IMatch, follow these steps:

1. **Launch the program.**

2. **Press Ctrl+W to launch the Database Wizard.**

3. **Direct IMatch to your CD drive.**

   One-hundred images take about three minutes to catalog.

   IMatch makes JPEG thumbnails on your hard drive. You could even use these thumbnails as e-mail attachments or desktop icons.

In Figure 2-8, you can see that IMatch rotates portrait image thumbnails automatically and also tells you that Photo CD files are multiresolution (MultiRes).

I can enter information about a file and the whole volume on CD.

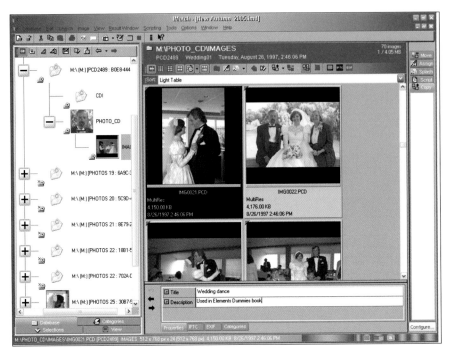

Figure 2-8: There's no real match for IMatch.

In Figure 2-9, I entered the photographer's credits in an IPTC field. Because you can't write to a Photo CD, IMatch's copyright info goes into the database; to "brand" an image file with copyrights, you need to use the Elements File⇨ File Info command. (Read all about that process in Book I, Chapter 2.)

Figure 2-9: Copyrights are easily added via IMatch's easy-to-use scripting language.

Why you can't enlarge digital images

When it comes to capturing images for printing or editing, I cannot overemphasize the need to capture exactly what you want at sufficient image resolution. You can make an image smaller and then use Filter⇨Sharpen⇨Unsharp Mask to make up for any blurriness.

You can't make a small image bigger.

A finite number of pixels are captured in an image, and Elements can somewhat intelligently discard unimportant pixels when you size-down a picture through *bicubic interpolation* — a noggin'-spinning term that means Elements analyzes the photo before shrinking it. However, neither you nor Elements nor the man in the moon can intelligently and artistically guess what color pixels should be added to an image to make it larger. This was the camera's job, and that time has passed. There will be occasions — lots of them — when you can't recapture a small image at higher resolution, and this is where a product such as PhotoZoom provides a good but not a complete solution.

Always use a high-resolution Photo CD image or a 6MP digital camera picture. But if that's not possible, try PhotoZoom.

PhotoZoom costs $129, available at www.benvista.com. Explaining how PhotoZoom works is complicated. Here's the short take:

1. PhotoZoom finds patterns and edges in the original picture.

2. PhotoZoom substitutes resolution-independent image information in a copy of the file wherever a pattern or edge is detected.

The result is quite good, even when you blow an image up by 600%. In contrast, the Elements Image Size⇨Bicubic Smoother option produces a blurrier image with tiny chunks in it. Figure 2-10 shows a tiny 72 ppi image, then up to 360 ppi using Elements' Bicubic Smoother, then up to the same size using PhotoZoom (an Elements plug-in accessed through the File⇨Save command). As you can see, the PhotoZoom image is crisper.

**Book II
Chapter 2**

Input from a CD

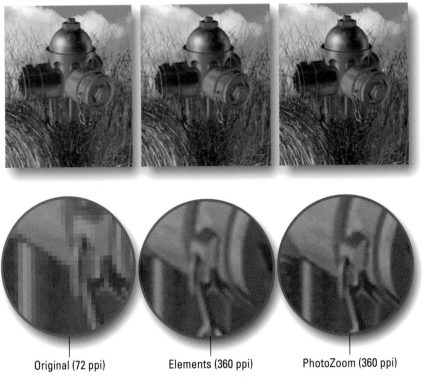

Original (72 ppi)   Elements (360 ppi)   PhotoZoom (360 ppi)

Figure 2-10: When high-rez isn't possible, try PhotoZoom.

Chapter 3: Input from a Scanner

In This Chapter

✓ **Getting the most from your scanner**

✓ **Understanding scanning resolutions and color settings**

✓ **Scanning using Elements**

✓ **Scanning using your hardware's software**

*S*canning is another way to create a digital image although this method is not your best option. Scanners get image data through *reflective* art: That is, light is bounced off the hard copy photo (or whatever is being scanned), and the scanner sort of gets the photo data second-hand. Digital cameras, in contrast, directly sample a scene; digital cameras (Chapter 1 of this mini-book) and Photo CDs (Chapter 2 of this mini-book) provide much better image colors.

However, when a scanner is your only option — say, when you don't have a film negative, which is often the case when you want to preserve family albums from decades ago — scanning an image can be a handy tool in your arsenal. Also, you can scan flat objects (such as fabric) and acquire more detail with better focus than snapping a picture. The scanner isn't just for photos, and its creative possibilities are limited only by your inventiveness.

This chapter takes you through two ways of scanning: within Elements, and using your scanner's software. Each method had advantages and disadvantages, which I explain here.

put type: Millions of

dimensions:

Examining the Anatomy of a Scanner

A scanner is a mini darkroom, with a lens system and circuitry. Despite the sophisticated thing it does, the mechanism is simple, and the technology is easy to grasp. If you're considering buying a scanner, the following sections take you through scanner options, care and cleaning, and finally how to use a scanner with Elements.

Scanner prices and features

Flatbed scanners are common and affordable (about $100 at an electronics big-box store). Don't buy a sheet-feed scanner, which is meant for printed documents and not for photos. You could bend and thus ruin a precious photo. Also, negative scanners are pricey and don't produce results as good as putting images on a Photo CD (see Chapter 2 of this mini-book). Try to find a scanner that has 24-bit depth, given your budget. If you feel like splurging, a 48-bit scanner costs from $250–$700 (from manufacturers such as Hewlett-Packard) and will sample with much more detail producing high-quality digital images. By the time this book hits the stores, 48-bit scanning might be affordable. Just remember that if you use Organizer to scan, 48-bit images are twice as large as conventional 24-bit scans, so the saved file size will be limited.

Scanners usually come in scanner/inkjet printer/fax combos. Okay, so fax capability is a little outdated; the last time I faxed something was when my stagecoach broke down. But seriously, having a scanner and your printer in one compact place on your desktop is very convenient.

Many scanners have a memory card slot so you can print directly from your digital camera — but then you'd miss the fun working in Elements. (For the scoop on memory cards, see Chapter 1 of this mini-book.)

Flatbed scanners are consumer models. Drum scanners are used commercially; a drum scan at a commercial print house will run you serious dollars.

Scanner prep: Before you scan

The only moving part of a scanner you need to mess with is the lid. Lift this to reveal the *platen,* which is the glass scanning surface.

The platen should be clean before you scan so you don't unwittingly record imperfections like dust, lint, and hair. Also, carefully wipe the object you want to scan to remove debris.

You can use window cleaner and lens wipes (from a camera store) to clean the platen. Spray the lens wipe and not the platen directly to clean it.

Do not wipe the platen with regular paper towels. They leave paper fibers on the platen — and your scanned image.

In Figure 3-1, you can see a photo of my scanner, which I used to document the scanning techniques in this chapter.

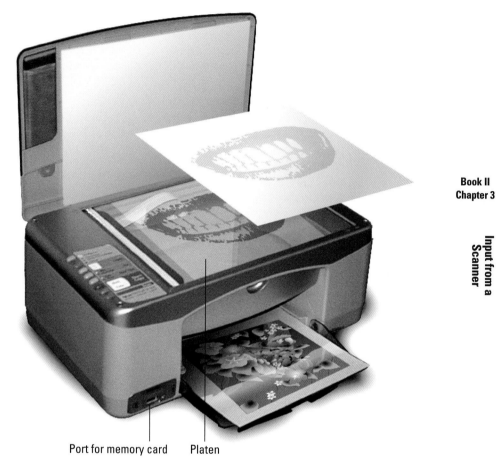

Port for memory card   Platen

Figure 3-1: Affordable scanners aren't much larger than the scanning surface.

Both Adobe Systems and scanner manufacturers label scanning resolution in *dots per inch (dpi),* which leads to some confusion because printer manufacturers measure output in dots per inch. However, printer dots are not equal to *samplers per inch* or the more common *pixels per inch* terminology, which is the correct phrase when describing digital image resolution. When describing a digital photo's dimensions to a pressman or the folks at a print store, be a geek and describe the file accurately using pixel resolution, not with this dots versus pixels ambiguity. You'll save money and a second trip.

Scanning tips

Now is a good time for timesaving and hardware-saving tips when scanning:

+ **Take the family photos out of the album to scan them.**

  The celluloid covers placed over images in albums impede a photo's brilliance (and probably have ten years of shmutz on them anyway). Additionally, you might want to buy an anti-static gun or brush from a camera shop to remove years' worth of static charge from heirloom photos. The action of removing a photo from its celluloid mount can cause dust particles to swarm to its surface. For heirloom photos mounted using fancy corners, there are no special steps or precautions.

+ **Make sure the photos are straight.** Elements can straighten photos if your scan is slightly askew, but it alters image data in the process. To prevent this potential loss, make sure that photos are straight on the platen before you scan.

  Buy a plastic geometry triangle at a school supply store to "T-up" your photos on the platen.

  If the border of a photo is crooked, you're sunk. Try your best to align the geometry in the photo to the platen; then straighten the photo and crop the border in Elements.

+ **Crop in the scanner.** Scans take a little time, so don't waste time scanning loosely. You want every scanned pixel to count, so consider cropping a portrait image to just that person's face.

  When the art of photography was in its infancy, photographers had a limited choice of lenses; thus, pictures of your great-grandmother probably include unnecessary background clutter. Crop in the scanner's preview window using the scanner's tools — just about every scanner comes with software that includes rules, guidelines, and cropping tools in the preview window.

+ **Get creative — but be tidy!** Scanners can sample real-life objects in addition to photos. Scans of textures can be used as Windows wallpaper and as resource files for projects you haven't even thought up yet. I've even scanned coffee beans; the detail was much better than I'd get using a camera although the scanner "lighting" of the scene was flat (and the house smelled terrific after scanning because scanners generate a little heat). You can also scan simple things like textiles — rough woven linen and muslin offer great texture. Textile patterns (prints) are usually copywritten, so don't scan (for example) a Hawaiian shirt or jazzy scarf for public display.

Before you decide to scan coffee, candy, or breakfast cereal, go to an art supply place and buy a sheet or two of thin unprepared acetate. (This kind isn't sanded; it's used for inking cartoon cels.) Put the acetate over the platen before you pour your Morning Crunchtastic cereal all over it. Flowers, candy, cereal — just about everything has lint and dust in it, ruining not only your scan but also messing up your scanner. Coffee bean dust and other debris are almost impossible to clean off the scanner platen without removing it.

Scanning through Elements Organizer

The software that comes with your scanner is probably better to use than Organizer. Still, you can use Organizer if you wish. The following section takes you through the particulars.

When you're all set to immortalize the family scrapbook, follow these steps:

1. **Close Elements Editor and run Organizer.**

2. **Click the camera icon to open a menu from which you choose From Scanner, as shown in Figure 3-2.**

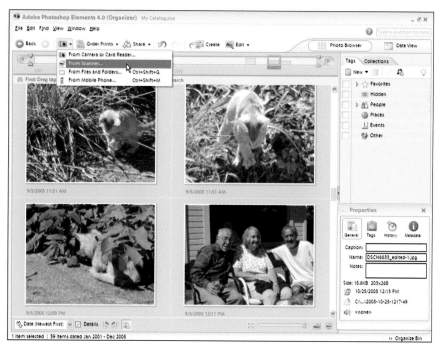

Figure 3-2: Start the scan here.

3. From the Scanner section of the Get Photos from Scanner window (see Figure 3-3), choose your scanning device.

The interface you get for scanning depends on the device (and device driver that accompanies the device) that you choose. I suggest that you use the manufacturer's device listed on the drop-down menu, and don't use TWAIN — a legacy driver — unless you own a pre-1995 scanner.

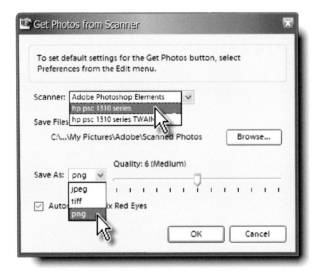

Figure 3-3: Choose your scanner and format here.

4. Choose the format in which to save the scan file.

Choose tiff or png from the Save As drop-down list. By default, saving scans as JPEG is chosen; however, JPEG loses information as you save.

The Quality slider disappears because PNG and TIFF file formats are uncompressed; they're 100 percent quality, so that's why the slider goes away.

You can have Organizer fix red-eye problems. Refer to Figure 3-3.

5. Click OK.

The following screen (see Figure 3-4) enables you to set the color depth of the images you scan. You have four choices here:

• **Color Picture:** I recommend that you go for color — enable the Color Picture radio button — even if your images are faded out sepia tones because some tone information in sepia tone images is lost if you scan in grayscale. Scan 'em in color and then use Hue/Saturation (Ctrl+U in Elements Editor) to remove the color cast. (Some people like sepia tone images, you know.)

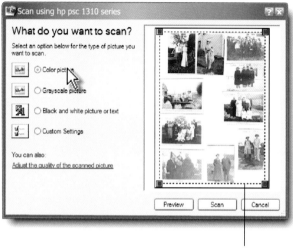

Cropping

Figure 3-4: Set the color depth here.

- **Grayscale Picture:** If an image is a true grayscale image, then scan in grayscale (select the Grayscale Picture radio button). Grayscale means the scan will be done using 256 brightness values and no color channels, and many of Elements' features won't work on the scan unless you choose Image⊅Mode⊅RGB Color, which changes the image data structure, but not the content of the scan. Here's a space-saving advantage: Your image will be one-third the size of a color image's saved file size.

- **Black and White Picture or Text:** Saving to black and white (1 bit per pixel) should be reserved for scanning text for optical character recognition (OCR) software such as OmniPage (www.nuance.com/omnipage) to convert to editable text.

  There's no reason to use this setting for Elements image work.

- **Custom Settings:** Select this radio button if you've already used the Adjust the Quality of the Scanned Picture option (located at the bottom of this window), which brings up the Advanced Properties box.

(See the upcoming Figure 3-5.) Basically, you have options only for Brightness/Contrast and scanning resolution. However, if you don't choose and then use Custom Settings, Elements uses the scanner's defaults.

Adobe Systems is not at fault with this less-than-straightforward procedure for doing something as simple as scanning. WIA (Windows Image Acquisition) is an application programming interface (API) that "lies" to applications to force scanning and other input devices to use hardware defaults.

Figure 3-5: Do nothing with Brightness and Contrast controls.

6. **In the Advanced Properties dialog box (see Figure 3-5), do nothing with the Brightness and Contrast controls.**

You'll get better results using Quick Fix mode (or Standard Edit) after the image has been saved to file.

Now here's the kicker. As you can see in Figure 3-4, I ganged up several vintage photos to scan them in one fell swoop. And I specified 600 pixels per inch resolution (refer to Figure 3-5) because old photos usually need extensive editing. *Hint:* Any image you want to edit — or just save for posterity — should be scanned larger than you'd ever want to print to preserve detail for future printing technology and to make editing easier. But as you can see, Organizer tells me (see Figure 3-6) that a full-page scan at 600 ppi is too large. Well, maybe for Elements, but not for my scanning software. At this point, you bite the bullet, use the preview window's crop box, and drag it to encompass only one image.

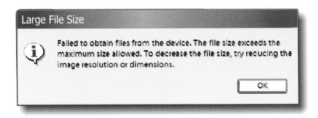

Figure 3-6: Click OK and move on.

Use the Browse button in the dialog box to choose where the image files should be saved. By default, they are saved to

```
C:\Documents and Settings\Your Computer LogIn Name\
    My Documents\My Pictures\Adobe\Scans
```

right next to your digital camera downloads.

In Figure 3-7, you can see that I cropped to only a single photo on the platen, and the scanning process begins. Organizer automatically puts scan thumbnails in your catalog; then it's your job to tag the scanned images to your collections (see Book I, Chapter 1).

Figure 3-7: Organizer scans the thumbnails.

After the scan is complete, Organizer shows you the image in the catalog window, where you can rotate the image if necessary. Also, Elements removes red-eye if you chose this option before scanning (refer to Figure 3-3). Figure 3-8 shows the scanning progress and lets you know that red-eye reduction was chosen and it's being performed.

If you want to scan more photos, you have to start the process again in Organizer clear at the beginning — there is no Continue button. That's strike two against scanning using Organizer (strike one being the limitation on scanning resolution).

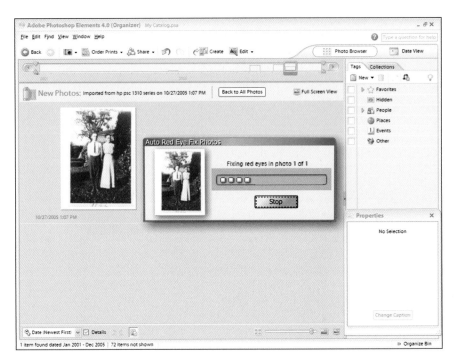

Figure 3-8: Your scan is complete.

Scanning Using Your Scanner's Software

The only disadvantage to using your scanner software is that scanned images won't automatically go into your Elements catalog. You have to use Organizer's Get Images feature and then tag them to use them in an Elements creation. However, this is a small price to pay. Too, you don't want large scans stored by default on your C: drive. (Every application seems to want to install to C:, and you'll eventually run out of space.)

First things first: Install your scanning software. It usually comes on a CD and installs just like any other Windows program. After installing, you should check the manufacturers' Web site for updated drivers, download them, and use the directions (online or in a text file) to install them. Scanner software is usually outdated by the time the scanner box has been sitting on a store shelf for more than a month.

After you're up and running, launch your scanning software. You can find the program via Start⇨Programs; the utility should look similar to the interface shown in Figure 3-9, with rudimentary tone and color controls. The biggest plus is that there's no theoretical limit to saved file size: Uncle Edwin, Aunt Eustace, and Binkie the Mule can be scanned to a file size that's 12MB, which is good for archiving and of greater resolution than needed for inkjet printing to 5" x 7". (175 to 225 ppi is just fine.)

Figure 3-9: Use your scanner's software.

Scanning resolution is relative; how many pixels per inch depends on the photo size and what you want to use the scan for. Scans for the Web don't need to be larger than 640 x 480 pixels, but heirloom photos should be scanned so they can be printed at least to 8" x 10". I usually scan to about an 80MB file for editing and archiving purposes, and then scale a copy of the image down for inkjet printing. ***Hint:*** In both Elements and your scanner's software, estimated file size is shown and can be reset.

The icing on the cake comes after you scan with your scanner's software (compared with Organizer). Hewlett-Packard scanning software — and probably yours, too — offers you a Continue button. Woo-hoo! Just change your cropping in the preview window, and before you know it, your family albums have been saved forever.

Preservation and Rights of Scanned Images

After editing the scans in Elements, follow these steps to preserve your scans and your work:

1. **Write the scans to CD twice, along with the original files.**

2. **Clear the files — with a clear conscience — off your hard drive.**

3. **For safe-keeping, drop the duplicate CD off at your folks or rent a bank safety deposit box.**

Don't risk keeping only one copy in your house or apartment!

In the Properties box in Organizer, the date, filename, scanner used, and file location on hard drive are saved. Still, you probably want more info for the sake of posterity and reference. Choose File➪File Info in Elements Editor to add people's names, date of the photo, location, and occasion. This info is embedded as an invisible text header in the photo, not merely added to Elements' database as a reference.

If you intend to publish scanned images, Web or otherwise, make sure that the photographer and/or subject (or his/her estate) okays it first. For example, the source images shown in this chapter were taken in 1922 and photographed by a family member (now deceased). My family is the rightful estate, so everything is cool.

Chapter 4: Input from Other Applications

*S*tepping back to take a gander at The Big Picture, Elements is not only a terrific image editor but a great design program, too. Part of its power comes from the fact that Adobe Systems published the standards for the PSD file format years ago; today, several other graphics programs can read and write the PSD format. Too, *Clipboarding* (copying and pasting) between Elements and other programs is functional. This chapter takes you through not only acquiring image elements created in other programs but also how well an exchange of image data — between Elements and some really hot applications — can work for you. You'll see how Painter (the Elements of the world of digital painting) and Xara Xtreme (a vector drawing program that thinks it's a bitmap program) can be used to enhance Elements compositions. I also show you how to use Right Hemisphere's Deep Paint 3, a free program, to create fresh and interesting Elements texture objects.

You can find all the files I use in this chapter at www. dummies.com/go/PhotoshopElementsAIOFD1e.

Importing Text from the Clipboard

Yup, you can import text via the copy-and-paste way from the standard Clipboard function of Windows and many other programs. However, Elements doesn't have a spell-checker, so unless you're an English major, I suggest that you proof your text in a word processor before you copy and paste that text into Elements. You don't want to e-mail a salutation to a friend who got kicked upstairs at work that reads, "Congartulations on the Big Pormotion!"

To import text to an Elements composition, follow these steps:

1. **Copy the text (Ctrl+C) from your text editor or word processor after running a spell-check.**

2. **With the Type tool in Elements, marquee-drag a box and then press Ctrl+V (paste).**

   The result is paragraph text, which I cover in Book VII.

3. **Specify the formatting — font, size, and color — by using the boxes and fields on the Options bar after highlighting the text (to select it for formatting).**

   Elements does not import formatting.

   Although Elements can read special characters such as em dashes and curly quotes, text editors don't usually specify these characters. Word processors, though — such as Word — can copy curly quotes, built fractions, and other special characters. Elements will paste them properly.

Putting It Together

Framing a Poem

To better examine how Elements does its text import thing, tag along to create a framed love sonnet.

1. **Open a background image.**

   I included the file Parchment.png as an illustration.

   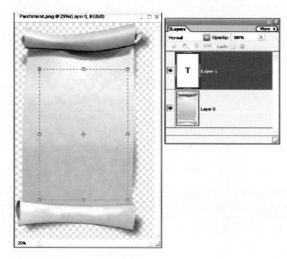

2. **Go online and find a poem that's in the public domain.**

   Avoid copyright issues.

   Or, load `BrowningSonnet.txt` in a text editor.

3. **Choose Edit⇨Select All (or press Ctrl+A), copy, and then close the text editor.**

4. **In Elements, choose the Type tool and then drag a marquee within the parchment. A new layer is created for the text and the parchment illustration remains intact.**

5. **Press Ctrl+V.**

6. **Select the text and format it.**

   a. *Insert your Type cursor anywhere in the text; then press Ctrl+A to select all.*

   b. *On the Options bar, choose*

   - **A classy font:** I used Windsor Condensed.

   - **Font size:** I went for about 60 points because it's a large image.

   - **Color:** Click the foreground color swatch on the Toolbox. From the Color Picker, choose your poison. I chose deep brown.

   If the text box doesn't fit the layout exactly, drag on a text bounding box handle. You're not smooshing the text itself but rather the container for the text.

7. **Make the text conform to the text container.**

   I intentionally made the parchment swoopy. To make the text more or less conform to the parchment shape

   a. *With the text selected, click the Warp Text icon, directly to the right of the Color swatch on the Options bar.*

   b. *From the Warp Text dialog box, choose Arch (for a rounded effect). Then drag the Bend slider to –6%, the Horizontal Distortion to +2%, and the Vertical Distortion to –5%, as shown here.*

   This bends the sonnet to conform to the parchment, as you can see here.

8. **Drag the text layer's thumbnail onto the New Layer icon on the Layers palette to duplicate it. Then click the original, lower text layer thumbnail.**

9. **Click the color swatch and choose white.**

10. **With the Move tool (V) chosen, press the keyboard down-arrow once and then press the right arrow.**

    You create an engraved text effect.

Book II
Chapter 4

Input from Other Applications

continued

continued

11. **Save the image as `Browning.psd` and keep it open.**

Text can be copied from an image layer and pasted into a word processor document. Follow these steps with the Type tool:

1. **Click an insertion point.**

2. **Press Ctrl+A to select all the text.**

3. **Press Ctrl+C to copy.**

To continue creating the sonnet illustration, close Elements. You need to go online to download and install a new application.

Installing programs while Elements or any other application is running is like putting an Elements finger in a light bulb socket (if Elements had fingers).

Applying Other Paint Programs with Elements

Deep Paint is an application that is a combination of Elements and Painter. In the following sections, you can download the free program and then use it to generate an eye-pleasing background for the parchment.

Deep Paint

Deep Paint, from Right Hemisphere, is excellent for making background images. It speaks the PSD file format, and you can paint with anything from liquid mercury to leaves.

Deep Paint is in version 4, but version 2 is free to download. (I wish more companies gave away the previous version of their software.)

Run (do not walk) to

`www.download.com/Deep-Paint/3000-2191_4-10398243.html`

This is a 58MB download, so you need a broadband connection, but a great freebie like this is the sort of thing that keeps the computer graphics community happy and grateful.

Install the program and then restart Elements (and reload `Browning.psd` from the preceding section).

Say you really like Elizabeth Barrett Browning's sonnet enough to print and frame it, 8" x 10" on an 8 ½" x 11" page.

**Book II
Chapter 4**

**Input from Other
Applications**

Putting It Together

Prepping an Elements File for Deep Paint

The `Browning.psd` design needs to be adjusted so it can be used in Deep Paint. (You can use my `Parchment.psd` file.)

1. **Right-click the image title bar and then choose Image Size.**

2. **In the Image Size dialog box, clear the Resample Image check box and then type** 9 **in the Height field.**

 continued

continued

That leaves two inches of background you'll add (and printers don't print clear to paper edges, anyhow). You'll notice that the image resolution decreases, but it's still higher than the recommended resolution for inkjet printing, so life is good.

3. **Click OK.**

4. **Right-click the image title bar and choose Canvas Size.**

   In the Canvas Size dialog box, increase the canvas to the same dimensions as inkjet paper, as shown here.

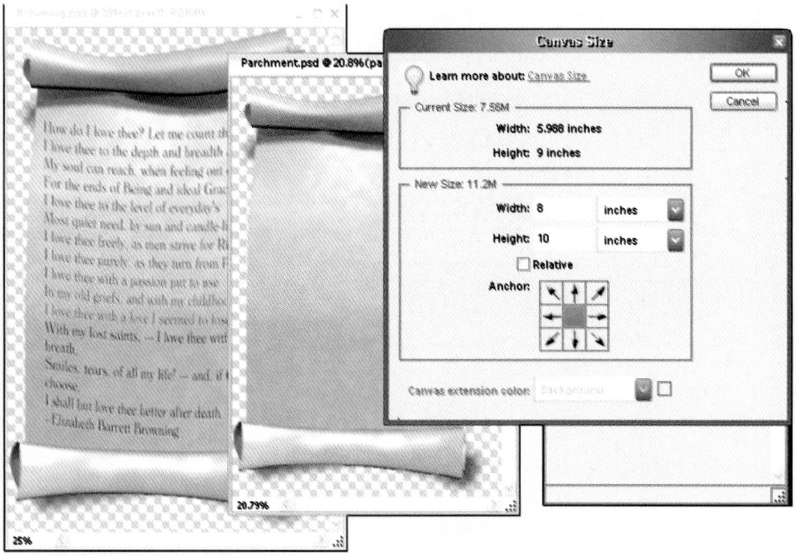

5. **Click OK.**

6. **Create a copy of the parchment:**

   One thing Deep Paint cannot do is read editable text in a PSD file, and it'd be a shame to convert the text to bitmap format. (You can presently change the type.)

   a.   *Right-click the image window title bar.*

   b.   *Choose Duplicate.*

   c.   *In the Duplicate Image dialog box, type **Browning.psd** in the As field.*

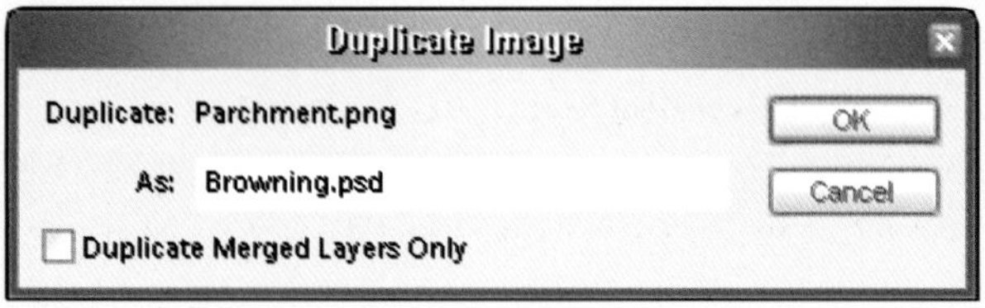

A new image window opens

7. **Delete the text layers in the duplicate image and save the file.**

8. **Launch Deep Paint.**

9. **In Deep Paint, open** `Browning.psd`**.**

10. **On the Control palette, click Layers and then lock the parchment layer.**

11. **Right-click the title and choose Add Layer Below.**

12. **Double-click the new layer title and name it** *stone*.

13. **Click the Supplies tab and choose Tiles from the drop-down list..**

14. **Choose Stone and then click the Parameters tab to the right.**

15. **Click the Behavior drop-down list and then drag the X Scale slider to 16, as shown here.**

    The Toolbox looks very similar to the one in Elements.

16. **With the Paint Bucket tool, click in the image window.**

17. **Right-click the parchment layer title, choose Add Layer Above, and name this layer** *ivy*.

18. **Click the Art Supplies tab and choose Ivy from the drop-down list.**

 continued

continued

19. On the Settings tab (Behavior), type 3.22 in the Scale X field.

20. With the Paintbrush tool, stroke ivy leaves around the bottom of the image window, as shown here.

21. Create a new layer on top of the ivy layer, add some butterflies using the Butterflies setting for the Brush tool, create a layer on top of the parchment, and stroke in about four more butterflies at the top.

    The maximum size for the Butterflies brush produces butterflies that are on the small size, but this can be fixed in Elements.

22. Choose File⇨Save As, save the file to PSD file format, ignore the warning box about saving lighting information, and close Deep Paint without saving.

Putting It Together

Finish the Scroll

It's time to bring your work back into Elements to add a final touch or two. Follow these steps:

1. Open the Deep Paint document and `Browning.psd` (the design with the text). With the Browning file you saved in the foreground, right-click the bottom type layer and choose Duplicate layer.

2. Choose the Deep Paint document as the target and then click OK.

3. Repeat this step with the top type layer.

   The text plops perfectly into position because the images are the same size, as you can see here. **Bonus:** The text is still editable.

4. Close the Browning file and then click the top butterflies layer on the Layers palette.

5. With the Lasso tool, select a butterfly and then press Ctrl+T to put the selected butterfly in Free Transform mode.

6. Lock the proportions by clicking the link icon on the Options bar; then enlarge the selected layer area by dragging on a corner bounding box handle.

   In this example, I'm enlarging the butterfly.

   If the butterfly is upside down (Deep Paint does this), hover the cursor around a corner bounding box handle until it turns into a bent arrow; then drag in any direction to rotate the butterfly.

7. Press Enter to apply the transformation and then press Ctrl+D (deselect). See the results in the following figure.

continued

continued

The text could use a little more distortion, but this can't be done without simplifying both text layers to non-text pixels.

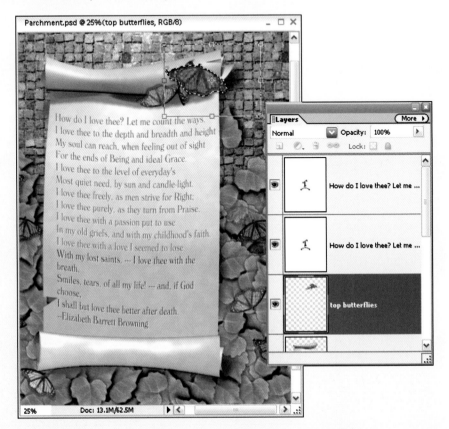

8. Make any final modifications to font choice and size if you so choose.

9. Right-click, one at a time, the text layer thumbnails on the Layers palette, and choose Simplify Layer. Then right-click the top text layer thumbnail and choose Merge Down from the contextual (pop-up) menu.

10. Choose Filter➪Distort➪Liquify. Then drag the Liquify filter box by its title bar to the right so you can see the image file in the workspace.

11. Drag the text toward the bottom a little to the left, as shown in the next figure, and then click OK.

12. Flatten the image so it becomes an ordinary bitmap image and other programs can load it (and your editing work is done, so saving without layers conserves file size), save it to PNG format (non-interlaced), and then print a copy for framing.

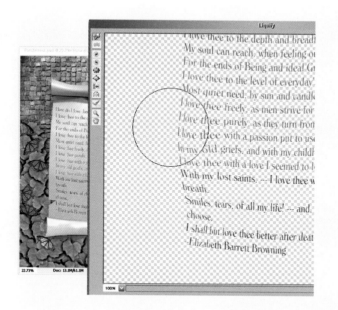

One good reason to import designs from Deep Paint is that its brushes look more fresh and original than Corel Painter's goodies. The clover Image Hose in Painter, for example, is getting overused and looks a little tired. Trick #1 to good design is to use programs that are off the beaten path.

In Figure 4-1, I brought a photo of a kid's go-kart into Deep Paint and painted some text by using the Candy brush. In Elements, I added a drop shadow to the candy layer. As you can see, the text not only looks 3-D (strokes overlap each other), but the composition looks unique.

Figure 4-1: Strive for originality when you create a composition.

Corel Painter

This is an overview section; I don't expect you to dash out and buy Painter, but I want to show you some interesting stuff. Like Deep Paint, Paint reads and writes PSD files, and you can paint with bitmaps.

Download a free 30-day trial of Painter IX at

www.corel.com/NASApp/cs/Satellite?pagename=Corel3/Downloads/Trials

I thought that this photo of the Villanueva Well is beautiful but needs a little more green and some orange to make it more appealing. In Painter, I created a new layer, used the Fronds Image Hose nozzle, and then stroked in some Poppies with its nozzle; see Figure 4-2. When I reopen this photo in Elements, I can move the poppies and fronds around by using the Move tool and put the layer in different blending modes. You can even erase some of the new foliage without altering the base image. Although it's not an image editor nearly as capable or simple to use as Elements, Painter's brushes excel at realistic renderings of traditional, physical media.

Figure 4-2: You play upon Painter's strengths and then use Elements to refine a composition.

Perhaps Painter's most remarkable feature lies in enabling you to create a very realistic painting from a photo. In comparison, the Elements Artistic filters, such as Watercolor, just don't have the authenticity. In Painter, you stroke over photo areas like you'd trace over a photo, and the result is a true hand-painted effect.

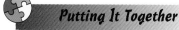

Putting It Together

Painting in Painter

The following steps show how to Clone Paint in Painter. (If you want to try them with my example, open `VillanuevaWell.tif` in Painter.) Follow these steps:

1. **Choose File⇨Clone.**

   A copy of the image appears in the workspace. Layers will be flattened in the copy.

2. **Choose the Brush tool from the Tools palette.**

3. **On the Brushes palette, choose the Cloners category and choose a medium for cloning.**

   For this example, I recommend the Chalk cloner.

4. **On the Brush Controls palette, create a tip with a size in proportion to the image file.**

   For the example image, I recommend an 18 pixel tip.

5. **Stroke in the image, following the geometry of the building.**

6. **After completely stroking the image, choose Effects⇨Apply Surface Texture and then choose the amount, softness, and lighting direction. I recommend these settings:**

   - 1.6 Softness
   - 35% Amount
   - 25% Shine
   - Lighting direction at 3 o'clock

   For additional effect, use a pale yellow for the lighting color; R:255, G:255, B:233 works well.

7. **Click OK and then press Ctrl+S.**

   Painter automatically creates a file called *Clone of MyFile.file extension*. In the following figure, you can see the results.

continued

Book II
Chapter 4

Input from Other
Applications

To make a photo look even more like a painting, filter it with the Cutout Artistic filter in Elements before you open it in Painter.

Xara Xtreme

Xara Xtreme is available for $79 at `www.xara.com/products/xtreme`. You can also download a fully functional trial version (about 22MB). It's a vector drawing program that also works well as a bitmap editor, and it can import an Elements PNG image with transparency (the background drops out).

 Putting It Together

Creating Fake Truck Signage

Okay, it's Silly Time, so read along to see how to put signage on an antique truck using Elements and Xara Xtreme; follow along with my file `Truck.png`.

1. With the Elliptical Marquee tool, drag an oval around the truck.

2. Right-click and choose Feather.

3. **Specify the number of pixels to feather the selection, and then click OK.**

   For this example, I recommend 25 pixels.

4. **Right-click and choose Layer Via Cut.**

5. **Choose the Background layer thumbnail on the Layers palette and then click the trash icon.**

6. **Press Ctrl+S and then clear the Save a Copy check box so Elements will save the transparency.**

   The figure here shows the feathered selection cut to a new layer.

7. **In Xara, press Ctrl+Shift+I to import the image.**

8. **Click the Lighting tool (the L with a light bulb icon on the Toolbox) and then click the Glow icon (the far right one) on the Toolbar.**

9. **Drag the left slider on the Toolbar all the way to the right to blur the glow to the maximum setting and then drag the right slider all the way to left to maximize glow density.**

   By default, the Glow effect is red. Change the color by clicking the glow with the Pick tool and then clicking yellow on the color strip.

10. **Choose the Rectangle tool, drag a rectangle around the truck, press the spacebar to toggle to the Pick tool (similar to the Move tool in Elements), and then press Ctrl+B to send the rectangle behind the truck image.**

11. **Click the Fill Gallery icon (the paint bucket) on the Toolbox and then browse for a good texture fill.**

    You can click the Get Fills button, and Xara will go online and import new fills. Xara is always posting bitmap fills for free.

12. **After you decide on a fill, drag its thumbnail on top of the black rectangle.**

    As you can see in the next figure, the glow around the truck image blends with the textured rectangle because Xara anti-aliases (see Book I, Chapter 3) both vectors and bitmap images.

13. **If you'd like to add text to the image, go for it with the Text tool.**

    If you want to use uneditable text, load `Fred's.xar` and copy it into the truck composition: Press Ctrl+A to select all, Ctrl+C, then close the window, press Ctrl+V, and then use the Pick tool to position the text.

continued

continued

Note: All text in `Fred's.xar` has been converted to curves, so don't worry about owning the typefaces I used.

14. **Scale the artwork to fit on the truck side by dragging a corner bounding box handle toward the center of the text.**

15. **Choose the Mould tool in perspective mode (on the Toolbox) and make the signage look like it's tilting at the same angle as the truck's side.**

    In the next figure, you can see that I made a guideline for myself.

16. **With the Transparency tool (the wine glass icon), drag diagonally in the signage and then choose Stained Glass mode on the Toolbar (equivalent to the Elements Multiply blending mode).**

    The signage in the final figure looks like it's reacting to the daylight and really looks painted.

17. **Press Ctrl+A (select all) and then press Ctrl+Shift+E to export the composition.**

18. **Choose the PNG file format and then choose True color as the Color Depth.**

19. **Click the Bitmap Size tab and pick a resolution for the copy.**

    I suggest 145; PNG files save image resolution, and there's no reason to scale the composition and distort pixel information.

20. **Click Export; and you're done.**

Multiply made with linear transparency

If you want to add an alternative element to the composition, you can add an Effect in Elements instead of a Xara texture background. Follow these steps:

1. **In Xara, click the background rectangle.**
2. **Press Delete.**
3. **Press Ctrl+A.**
4. **Press Ctrl+Shift+E.**
5. **Choose True color+alpha.**
6. **Export to PNG.**

Don't be surprised by the empty background when you open the image in Elements. A Xara True color+alpha bitmap has a transparent background, just as you saved the image.

Book III
Color Correction

The 5th Wave   By Rich Tennant

THE TRAGEDY OF POORLY WRITTEN
SLINKY DOCUMENTATION.

You don't have to let a tint taint an otherwise perfect picture. Take a stand. Say "Halt!" to those hateful hues. This mini-book shows how to correct the colors in a picture by using both Quick Fix and manual techniques. I share with you the tricks for adjusting image exposure to get crisp whites; deep, rich shadows; and other fascinating, provocative imagery. And if you want to turn back the clock (photographically speaking, of course), check out the section on creating a vintage photo.

Chapter 1: Correcting Image Exposure

*T*he human eye is more sensitive to the brightness quality in an image than color, and so a good basic area to begin when correcting and enhancing your photos is with the Elements brightness features (also known as value, lightness, brightness, and luminosity).

Fortunately, Elements doesn't ask that you plunge right into brightness correction head first. Plenty of auto-correct buttons are at your disposal, and this chapter takes you through both auto and manual finessing of photo exposure.

All sample files that I use (and you can, too) in this chapter can be found at www.dummies.com/go/ PhotoshopElementsAIOFD1e.

Using the Quick Fix Mode to Correct Exposure

The Editor module of Elements — the main topic of this book — has a toggle to a mode known as *Quick Fix*. You click the button at the top right of the interface (as shown in the upcoming Figure 1-1) to access this tool. When you do, most of your painting and editing tools go away. At your command are new controls intended to revive an image's exposure, with additional features used to adjust the following settings:

✦ **Hue:** This is the distinguishing characteristic of a color.

✦ **Saturation:** This is the oomph in a color; black and white photos have no saturation, for example.

✦ **Color temperature:** Indoor photography casts a little red, and outdoor photography casts blue.

✦ **Tinting:** This acts very much like the Hue control.

All of the above terms are covered in detail within the context of Quick Fix mode in Book II, Chapter 2.

To use Quick Fix in Auto mode, you just click the Auto buttons.

You won't always get a better image using Quick Fix. Auto does not equate to *correct,* and Quick Fix only estimates. However, if you click any Auto button and the results are worse than the original, just click the Reset button. If you drag sliders and mess up, click Auto again to enable the Reset button.

Mistakes made in Quick Fix can be undone in the Standard Edit mode by pressing Ctrl+Z.

To use the Quick Fix feature to correct exposure, follow these steps:

1. **Open the photo you want to correct.**

   If you want to follow along with the example, open `PoorLighting.png`.

2. **Click the Quick Fix button on the toolbar.**

   The Quick Fix window opens, as shown in Figure 1-1.

3. **From the View drop-down list at the bottom of the window, choose Before and After (Portrait).**

4. **Click the Auto button in the Smart Fix field in the General Fixes panel.**

   Elements restores contrast to the image. However, Auto Fix might introduce other problems to the image. For example, when you use Auto Fix to correct the Before image in the example, it restores contrast to the image, but the image now has a neon glow, and the color casting is way heavy into the reds.

5. **If Auto Fix corrected your exposure problem, you're finished. Otherwise, click the Reset button above the right image to manually fix the problem.**

6. Click the Auto button next to Contrast.

Auto Constrast fixes the image's contrast only, while Smart Fix Auto attempts to correct every aspect of a photo.

The image improves dramatically. For this image, adjusting shadows, highlights, or *midtones* (the tone area in an image where much facial information resides) is now unnecessary, but it's still a little too warm, too red.

7. Drag the Hue slider a little to the right.

Doing this moves the image out of the red hue and into yellows, toward realistic skin tones. You don't need to move all the sliders in Quick Fix; instead, you tweak only image properties that are problematic.

8. If the image is blurry, click the Auto button in the Sharpen field.

You're done. Figure 1-1 shows an image before and after it was edited using only Auto Contrast and Auto Color.

**Book III
Chapter 1**

**Correcting Image
Exposure**

Figure 1-1: Auto-correction is helpful but isn't a cure-all for every sick image.

Correcting Exposure with the Levels Command

The human eye is more sensitive to brightness values (tonal information) than color mismatching. Aften, correcting exposure through adjusting tones brings image colors more into line.

An image has 256 different levels of brightness, from 0 (Black) to 255 (White). The Levels command (Ctrl+L) enables you to smoothly redistribute tone values, adding contrast (Input Levels controls) or reducing contrast (Output Levels controls). In the Levels dialog box, as shown in Figure 1-2, you can use three different sliders to adjust brightness:

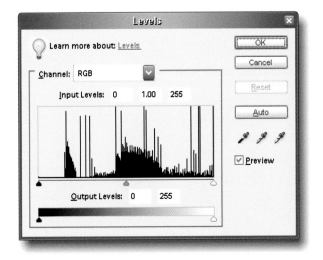

Figure 1-2: Use commands here to adjust brightness.

✦ **Input Black Point slider:** Drag the Input Black Point slider to the right, for example, and Elements redistributes the brightness in an image to give dark image pixels even denser values and also re-maps all the brightness values in the image in the process to create a more eye-pleasing image.

✦ **Input White Point slider:** Drag the Input White Point slider to the left, and Elements scales all the values in the image to create a whiter-than-white, contrast-crisp photo.

✦ **Input Midpoint slider:** Use this slider to enhance areas of most detail in an image. Drag it a little to the right to draw out facial details (increasing contrast in only the midtone range), or drag it to the left when a person's face in an image has harsh shadows.

You can balance an image's tones by using the Levels Auto feature, adjusting the manual black and white point settings, using Adjustment Layers, and adjusting single channel Levels, which I cover one at a time in the sections that follow. You can choose which method to use, depending on the photo problem.

If you want to follow along with the examples in the following sections, open the `GoldenGate.png` file. As you can see, ocean mist has created a haze in the image, which has okay color and composition, but it's impossible to see "black blacks" and "white whites" in the image. The photo needs more distinct tone ranges. Try using the Auto Levels and then take a manual approach to tonally enhancing the photo.

Auto-adjusting levels

The Auto Levels command works its magic by *clipping out* (discarding) ten percent of the top brightness values and ten percent of the shadow region and then reassigning adjusted tone values to the entire image (although you cannot change this percentage). To use this command, open your image and then follow these steps:

1. **Press Ctrl+L to display the Levels dialog box.**

   You see the image's *histogram* (the black readout that looks like a stereo's equalizer), which shows the number of pixels at a specific brightness value in the image. For example, in Figure 1-3, the histogram reveals no pixels at the black points.

Book III
Chapter 1

Correcting Image
Exposure

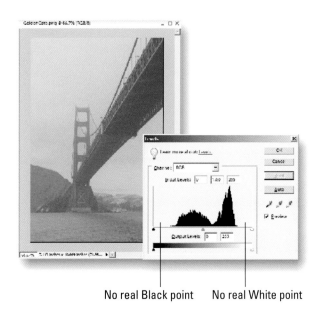

No real Black point   No real White point

Figure 1-3: No black pixels at the original levels.

2. **Click the Auto button.**

The image immediately snaps up. In Figure 1-4, you can see that the Auto Levels command has removed the haze that was in the original photo.

Unfortunately, the Auto process introduces a little color casting with many images, so a trip to the Quick Fix color temperature feature might be in order with images of your own. For more on how to use this feature, see Book II, Chapter 2.

Figure 1-4: Using the Levels Auto button can remove the haze in a photo.

In Figure 1-3, the closeup of the Levels histogram on the right reveals a saw-toothy profile. What Levels did was reduce or eliminate brightness values neighboring other values that it estimated were really important, thereby increasing contrast on a very subtle level. The effect of this inter-tone-contrasting is a good one for images whose overall contrast is poor, but there's also a way to add contrast/reduce image haze without adding the Auto pinch of contrast.

Setting a black point and a white point manually

Here's how to manually set the black point, white point, and midpoints in your image:

1. **Press Ctrl+L to display the Levels dialog box.**

2. **Drag the Input Black Point slider to the right until it reaches some pixels on the histogram's low end.**

3. **Drag the Input White Point slider to the left, into some pixels on the histogram's high end.**

4. **Click Reset.**

   Now you see what those tiny eyedroppers are for.

5. **Press F8 to display the Info palette. Click the eyedropper in the upper-right quadrant and choose Grayscale from the flyout menu so the Info palette tells you brightness values.**

6. **Choose the Set Black Point eyedropper (see Figure 1-5).**

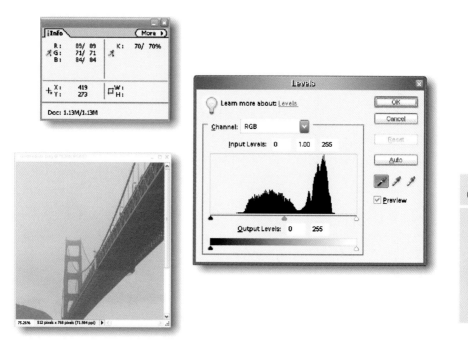

Book III
Chapter 1

Correcting Image Exposure

Figure 1-5: Use the Set Black Point eyedropper to set the darkest part of an image.

7. **Hover over the underside of the bridge until the Info palette indicates your cursor is over the highest numbers (the darkest point, the highest amount of black — it's labeled *K* on the Info palette) in the image and then click.**

   Your image improves in shadow areas, and the Levels histogram changes.

8. **Choose the Set White Point eyedropper (the far-right eyedropper icon in the Levels dialog box), then hover your cursor over the image until the Info palette's grayscale field reads the lowest value out of any values in the image, and then click.**

For the example, hover over the clouds at the top left until the Info palette indicates your cursor is over the highest numbers (the lightest point) in the image and then click. As shown in Figure 1-6, you can now evaluate a second result of using the Levels command.

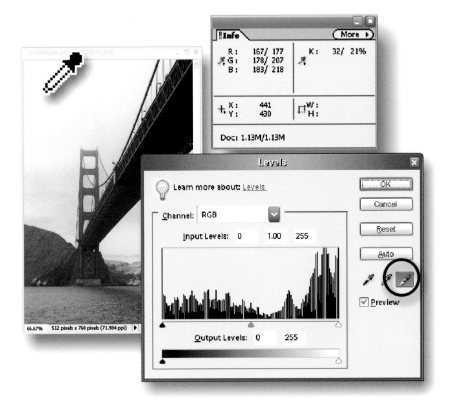

Figure 1-6: Professionals lean toward the eyedropper method of tone-balancing for its precision.

Changes you make to the tones in an image are *progressive* — that is, you create changes based upon changed visual information. You can't increase contrast using Levels, for example, and then expect to restore the image by then decreasing contrast. Elements re-maps, and in the process, eliminates pixel tones when you tell it to increase contrast. You can't undo the changes except by undoing them by using the Undo History palette (F10) or by pressing Ctrl+Z.

Using Adjustment Layers to Correct the Tones in Part of an Image

To adjust the tones in only part of an image, you can use an Adjustment layer in Levels mode. You click that funny MoonPie icon on the Layers palette, choose

Levels, and then adjust the overall image so it looks right using any of the Quick Fix, Auto Levels, or manual Levels techniques (all of which are described earlier in the chapter). After you make those adjustments, you use the Brush tool to paint using black to restore areas that look wrong because of the Levels command. Your painting does not permanently affect the image — you can undo by painting white into the areas you painted black — and you then finalize your selective tone corrections by flattening the image (see Book I, Chapter 4).

Follow these steps to use an Adjustment layer to partially correct an image:

1. **Click the Adjustments Layer icon on the Layers palette (see Figure 1-7), and then from the drop-down list that appears, choose Levels.**

   The Levels dialog box pops up.

2. **Drag the Input White Point slider to the left until it's beneath some histogram pixels, as shown in Figure 1-7.**

3. **Drag the Input Black Point slider to the right until it's beneath some histogram pixels, as shown in Figure 1-7.**

Figure 1-7: The Adjustment layer should have the final levels for the foreground.

4. Click OK to close the Levels dialog box.

5. Choose the Brush tool, press D (default colors; the brush paints with black now), and choose the brush size and opacity.

For this example, choose the 200 pixel tip from the Options bar, and set the Opacity to 50%.

6. Restore some of the original Levels values.

For the example, click — don't drag — the clouds in the image; you don't need to drag with as large a brush tip as you're using. As you can see in Figure 1-8, you're undoing the Levels adjustment in the clouds area. Click again in the clouds to add tone variation. Click once or twice more in different cloud areas; because the brush is set to partial opacity, it gradually and progressively restores the original levels in areas where you click.

Figure 1-8: Restore the original levels of the clouds by applying black.

7. On the Layers palette, right-click over the levels thumbnail — either the paint preview or the histogram icon — and choose Flatten Image from the contextual menu.

Flattening applies the Adjustment layer to the image. The image becomes non-layered (and thus can be imported to any application), and you now know a third method for correcting exposure using Levels.

Adjustment layers don't permanently affect an image. It's only when you merge that layer with its associated image layer that you create a change. So you can paint with black to restore image areas, paint with white to restore changes, and even hide the adjustment layer by unchecking its eye icon on the Layers palette to view the original image before committing to changes. And if you'd like to refine the adjustment, double-clicking the histogram thumbnail on the Layers palette displays the Levels command (or other adjustment, such as Hue).

Correcting a Single Tone Channel

Photos you take are almost always in RGB mode. Red, green, and blue (RGB) components contribute, at different levels, to all the colors you see onscreen. Often on overcast days, a photo you'll take is tonally eye-pleasing in foreground areas, but trees or the sky in the background appear dull. If you could tweak the green channel (component) of the RGB image, for example, the trees take on more color and life because the tones are then greater in contrast.

Contrast is linked to color because brightness is a component of color, as are hue and saturation.

You can tune the levels of a single color channel in Elements by choosing that channel in the Levels command, leaving alone foreground areas that don't possess much of that color. You choose the channel in Levels and then lower the white point (adding brightness to this color) and decrease the output black point. In the following example, you can experiment with Output Levels to demonstrate its purposefulness.

If you want to follow along with the example in the following steps, open the Well0017.png file and follow these steps to bring out the green in the trees and grass by remapping only the tones in the image's green channel.

Follow these steps to correct a single tone channel:

1. Press Ctrl+L to open the Levels dialog box.

2. From the Channel drop-down list, choose the tone channel you want to correct.

3. **Drag, one at a time, the Input Black Point and White Point sliders toward the midpoint.**

Contrast in the green channel increases, and the Levels histogram shows the changes.

For the well example, choose the Green channel. After you make your selection, the histogram changes. Drag the Input White Point slider to the left a little. Alternatively, you can enter a value in the far-right Input field to brighten the channel a little. 236 works with this image, but use your eye to evaluate the amount for your own images.

4. **On the Output Levels slider, drag the Black Point slider a little to the right.**

The Output field is used to decrease contrast. By widening the shadows region, you allow more image detail to become visible — this is true for all images, and Output adjustment can be used for all color channels as well as the RGB composite. See Figure 1-9.

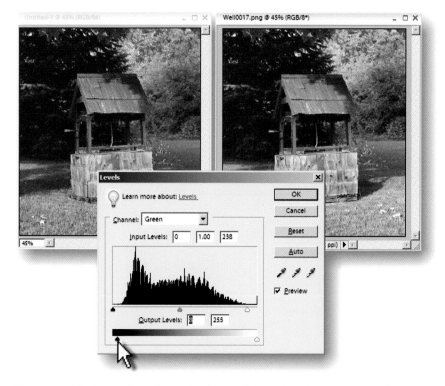

Figure 1-9: The Green channel contains the tone information about the trees and grass.

When you decrease the black or white points in an image, you decrease contrast. Black is the result of no color contribution from a color channel, and white is the total contribution of a color channel. And there's no room for subtle variations in tone at these absolute ends of the tonal range.

5. Switch to the RGB channel and then add some contrast using the Input sliders.

Often, the overall image needs some tone finessing after adjusting a single color channel.

The image is now greener where it should be, but the tonal scheme of the overall image is a little messed up. The trees are green but washed out. To fix this

a. *Choose the RGB Channel from the drop-down menu.*

b. *Drag the Input midtone slider to about .80, which adds contrast to the midrange, where much visual information pertaining to the leaves is stored.*

c. *Drag the White Point slider to the right, to about 233.*

d. *Press Enter.*

As you can see in the before and after images in Figure 1-10, the after image is crisper but also has a healthier green in the right areas. Notice also that the well, which contains very little to no green color component, has more contrast, but it's still brown. And the sky peeking through the trees is unaffected, and that orange branch is still orange.

**Book III
Chapter 1**

**Correcting Image
Exposure**

Figure 1-10: Adjusting a color channel's levels affects only the contrast in areas that have the color.

You need to know how to read a histogram so that you can better detect what's wrong with an image before using the Levels command. In the next section, you find out how to decipher a Histogram palette.

Interpreting the Histogram Palette

The Histogram palette is sort of like the Info palette: It does nothing to change an image but instead gives you clues. In the case of the Histogram palette, these clues pertain to the amount of color and brightness in an image or within a selection you create.

In the steps to follow, you find out how to analyze a histogram. For the example, I chose an image that's tonally correct (JulianTheSailor.png) so that you can better see what's right with the image. In this way, you can evaluate the tonal scheme of your own images to get a better idea of what needs correcting.

Follow these steps to check an image's colors and brightness:

1. **Choose Window⇨Histogram and then click the rotating arrows icon.**

   Doing this displays the uncached Refresh readout. Elements *caches* (stores in memory) image info, but you want an up-to-date readout and not one previously stored in system RAM (memory).

2. **Analyze the image's colors in the histogram to determine whether you need to adjust the contrast.**

   For example, if your image looks dull, the histogram displays a plateau with no peaks or valleys (peaks indicate a high population of pixels in an image at a particular brightness level; valleys indicate a deficiency of pixels at a specific brightness level), and the image needs contrast.

   Use your eye to tell you about the image's colors before looking at the histogram to confirm your suspicions. In the example, the histogram says there's some deep colors (the background), a lot of color in the upper midtones (the bright Hawaiian shirt), and not a lot of highlights. The shirt's white floral pattern — a small part of the whole image — accounts for most of the image's overall brilliance; the histogram shows a sparsity of highlights. Additionally, the color pixel distribution in the image makes gradual — not abrupt — transitions; the histogram is smooth — no spikes or anything. So you conclude that contrast does not need to be adjusted.

3. **Choose Luminosity from the Channel drop-down menu in the Histogram palette and then analyze the luminosity (brightness) of the image.**

If the image looks good with lots of shadow areas and few highlights, the histogram will bear you out, showing more pixels at shadow levels than at highlight levels. The inverse holds true; a photo of a blue sky with fluffy clouds will show high luminosity levels in the upper ranges, with few at lower levels.

As you can see in the lower histogram in Figure 1-11, there are a lot more deeper tones than lighter ones, which is perfectly appropriate for the image. *Luminosity, brightness, lightness,* and *value* are mostly synonymous. There's a good amount of brightness (Julian's shirt), and all's well with the luminosity of the image.

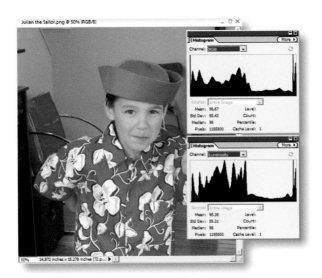

Figure 1-11: This is a good histogram of a well-exposed image.

4. **Click-drag in the center of the histogram to choose the midtones.**

Look at the Percentile field to determine what percentage of image pixels are midtone in brightness.

In the example, the Percentile field tells you that more than half the pixels in the image are midtone in brightness, which is a mark of a well-exposed image. In your own images, look for a high percentage of pixels in the midtones — most image detail in people photography lies in midtones, except for novelty photos, such as a full moon in a dark sky or a close-up of a bunch of balloons on a brilliant day.

Equally important in your own image evaluation is knowing what a histogram of a lousy image looks like. Figure 1-12 shows an image that's visually irretrievable, and the histogram confirms it — the image is practically devoid of pixels that have midtone and highlight brightnesses. I suggest reshooting such an image — Elements can't revive the dead, you know. I dragged in the shadows in the histogram, and the palette reported that almost 60% of the image pixels are in shade.

Figure 1-12: A poorly lit image doesn't have many midtone or highlight pixels.

Putting It Together

Enhancing an Average Image

The following steps take you through the techniques needed to enhance an average image — in which the tones are neither excellent nor an abomination. Open `BusinessGuy.png` and then follow these steps to improve the image:

1. **Press Ctrl+L to open the Levels dialog box.**

2. **With the Black Point eyedropper, click a very deeply colored area of the guy's hair, near his sideburn.**

3. **Choose the White Point eyedropper and click over the white in the guy's shirt.**

4. **Click the Midpoint eyedropper, click the guy's lapel, and then click OK.**

   As you can see in the figure, the image has snapped up, his flesh is a realistic (but not perfect) color, and the image haze is gone.

Note: I don't recommend this step for most images because it's rare that you'll take a picture containing perfectly neutral (equal amounts of R, G, and B) gray areas, but this guy's jacket is an exceptionally neutral color.

You defined a black, white, and midpoint tone for the image. It's ready for fine-tuning now.

5. **To lighten the guy's face, click the Quick Fix button and then drag the Lighten Shadows slider a little to the right. Then, to neutralize the red in his face, drag the Hue slider a tad to the right so that the guy's flesh has more yellow in it.**

   Lightening the shadow areas reveals more detail in the guy's face.

continued

continued

6. **Click the Standard Edit mode button.**

The concrete background is a little green, but you want to keep the fleshtone and overall tone-balancing work you've done.

7. **Click the Adjustment Layer icon, choose Levels, choose the Green channel, and then drag the Input midtone slider to the right to about 0.78. Click OK.**

The background is a neutral color now, but the business guy is too magenta.

8. **Press Ctrl+A, and then Alt+Backspace, and then Ctrl+D.**

You restored the whole image; the Levels icon on the Layers palette is black. By adding white, you reveal the leveled, neutral cement in the image while preserving the color and tone-balanced guy.

9. **Press X to swap foreground/background colors.**

10. **Using the Brush tool, paint white over the concrete areas.**

As you can see in the figure, the concrete changes tone and color, but the business guy remains as well adjusted as our economic atmosphere allows at this time.

11. **Right-click over the histogram thumbnail to access the contextual menu and then choose Flatten Image. If this were your own image, you'd press Ctrl+S to save it.**

Chapter 2: Improving Color Balance

In This Chapter

- ✔ **Using Quick Fix Saturation and Color Temperature controls**
- ✔ **Replacing a color**
- ✔ **Creating a vintage photo**
- ✔ **Working with color variations**
- ✔ **Using color creatively**

*I*n Chapter 1 of this mini-book, I cover the various methods for correcting the exposure — the *brightness values* — in several images. However, an image has additional traits, such as hue, saturation, and color temperature. This chapter shows how to apply color correction to an image that you've already tonally corrected; after you master color correction, you're well on your way to photo-perfection.

All sample files that I use (and you can, too) in this chapter can be found at `www.dummies.com/go/ PhotoshopElementsAIOFD1e`.

Adjusting Color Quickly

The simplest way to adjust a photo's color in Elements is by using Quick Fix mode. From the Standard Edit mode, you click the Quick Fix button at the top right of the interface and then click the Auto button in the Color field. Many times, this is enough to correct your image.

If using Auto doesn't do the job, try manually adjusting the hue, saturation, and other controls. An image usually needs only one adjustment, though, so you don't always need to fuss with all the options. In Figure 2-1, you can see all the controls at your disposal in Quick Fix mode. Stay tuned for more goodies in the Elements menus that can be used, which I explain in this chapter.

Figure 2-1: The Quick Fix panel is devoted mostly to color correction features.

Quick Fixing an Image's Colors

The Quick Fix mode of Elements Editor is an easy, fast route to color correction; no color theory education is required. However, you *do* need to know which Quick Fix control does what (refer to Figure 2-1):

✦ **Saturation:** This puts oomph in a color; black and white photos have no saturation, for example.

✦ **Hue:** This the distinguishing characteristic of a color. Blue, green, and other words that we call colors are hues.

✦ **Temperature:** Indoor photography casts a little red, and outdoor photography casts blue.

✦ **Tint:** This acts very much like the Hue control.

For the following example, I chose an image (`Scarecrow.png`) that's the correct *exposure* (the brightness values are correct), but the indoor lighting made the scarecrow in the photo blush. Indoor lighting color casting is a job for Quick Fix's color temperature control. Additionally, the scarecrow is *overly saturated* — the colors have too much presence.

Follow these steps to fix the colors in your image:

1. **Click the Quick Fix mode button on the top right of the Options bar.**

2. **Choose Before and After from the View drop-down list at the bottom left of the interface.**

3. **If your image is too juicy or too pale, you need to adjust the amount of saturation. Drag the slider to the left to desaturate or drag the slider to the right to increase saturation.**

   The example image is a little too saturated. Drag left on the Saturation slider until the After (right) pane looks a little more realistic when compared with the Before (left) pane.

4. **If your image is color casting, you need to adjust the temperature. Drag the slider to the left to make the image cast colder (indoor photography often needs toning down), or right to make the image warmer (outdoor photography frequently needs warming up).**

   For the example, drag the slider to the left until the background in the image is a little warm but predominantly a neutral gray. See Figure 2-2.

**Book III
Chapter 2**

**Improving
Color Balance**

Figure 2-2: Saturation and color temperature fix the most visible problem in this photo.

Although the Hue and Tint controls are not needed for the scarecrow picture, you might need them for your own photos:

✦ Drag the Hue slider to the left to cycle the image through violet, blue, and finally cyan. Note that Hue affects the entire image, and the results are usually unpredictable. Dragging right cycles the hues to orange, yellow, green, and finally to cyan.

✦ The Tint slider produces more predictable results than using Hue. Drag left to cast the image green, and drag right to cast the photo into magenta. Note that the Tint slider corresponds to Temperature offering complementary color variations.

Using the Replace Color Command

For the scarecrow example, no amount of color temperature twiddling will balance the background without ruining the scarecrow's colors because color temperature is a global adjustment, and you need a local adjustment feature to neutralize the image background and not the scarecrow. So you selectively replace the background color. Click the Standard Edit button to move to Elements Editor's other module. By doing this, you accept the changes you made in Quick Fix in the previous section. Choose Image⇨Adjust Color⇨ Replace Color from the main menu.

1. **With the Eyedropper, click over the background.**

   The preview window shows white for chosen areas.

2. **Increase the Fuzziness (the sensitivity of the eyedropper) until most of the background is white.**

   The Sensitivity feature is excellent for separating solid background colors from the foreground, which usually consists of varied and contrasting colors.

   In the example, do not let the black scarecrow silhouette display any white, however; ease off on the Fuzziness if this happens.

3. **With the Eyedropper + tool, click in any remaining background areas that show black.**

4. **Drag the Saturation slider so that the new color displayed in the Replacement field looks appropriate for the photo.**

   You can see your proposed changes in the image window. (Scoot the Replace Color dialog box out of the way if you need to.)

   For the example, drag the Saturation slider to –98, as shown in Figure 2-3. Then click OK.

5. **Occassionally, more than one color in an image needs replacement. If this is the case, pay a second (or third, or fourth) trip to Replace Color.**

Figure 2-3: The Replace Color command is your one-stop shop for altering the color of only a part of an image.

Believe it or not, the scarecrow's tunic is forest green, but it looks black because of the influence of red in the original photo. Choose Image⇨ Adjust Color⇨Replace Color again.

6. This time, change the hue of part of the image.

Replace Color is good for more than Saturation replacement; you can change the hue of an image area, too.

For the example, click the tunic. The scarecrow's nose is deep green, and the Replace Color command will fix this, too.

a. Adjust the Fuzziness.

b. Add to the tunic by using the Eyedropper + tool.

c. Drag the Hue slider all the way to the left, drag the Saturation slider to about +29, and drag the Lightness slider to +3.

d. Click OK.

Don't overdo it, or flat areas of completely saturated color will appear in the image *(color clipping)*. See Figure 2-4.

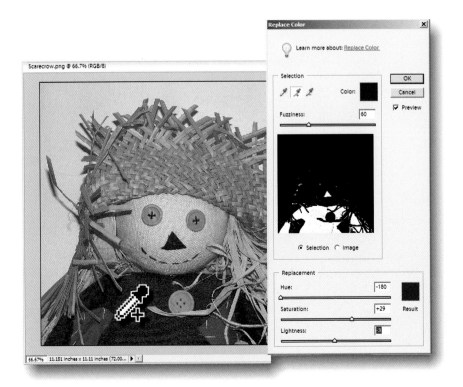

Figure 2-4: Most of the time, you can nudge a "no show" color to a more visible one by using the Hue, Saturation, and Lightness controls.

Creating Special Effects with Color

Hollywood special effects people often create *sepia tones* (predominantly brown images) to make a recent picture look 100 years old, and you can do this, too. The trick is to remove the saturation, creating a grayscale image, and then colorize it by using the Hue/Saturation command (Ctrl+U). And you're not limited to just using brown; you can create steel tones (shades of blue), burgundy-toned images . . . you name it. Hue/Saturation is a step up from using the Quick Fix Hue and Saturation features because you have more control and power.

The How To palette includes a script for creating an old-fashioned image, but you can't create images of different tints by running it.

Using the Hue/Saturation command

If you want to follow along with the example, open `TheLadyInRed.png`. Follow these steps to create a sepia tone image:

1. **Press Ctrl+U to display the Hue/Saturation dialog box.**

2. **Select the Colorize check box. Then drag the Hue slider to 20, the Saturation slider to 37, and the Lightness slider to 0. These values will turn any photo to sepia.**

   The resulting example image is shown in Figure 2-5.

3. **When you're satisfied with your changes, click OK to colorize the image.**

Figure 2-5: Use different Hue settings to create images of different tints.

Using layers to selectively colorize an image

Adjustment layers (discussed in Chapter 1 of this mini-book) can be used to create a visually intriguing image. In the following steps, you find out how to apply the Hue/Saturation command to an Adjustment layer. Using the example image of the preceding section (TheLadyInRed.png), you make everything except the woman's face a cool tone.

To selectively colorize an image, follow these steps:

1. **Click the Adjustment Layer icon (the MoonPie icon on the Layers palette) and then choose Hue/Saturation from the drop-down list.**

   The command box opens.

2. **Mark the Colorize check box, drag the Hue slider to the value for the color you desire, and then click OK.**

   I used a hue of 211 in this example to get a steel blue.

3. **Press Ctrl+A, D (default colors), and then Alt+Backspace.**

   In the example, the lady is back to red again because the Adjustment layer is completely black, creating no color changes as far as hue and saturation go. Now, you paint with white to restore the colorize command on the Adjustment layer, thus creating a steel-tone-with-full color-areas effect in the image.

4. **Press X (swap foreground/background colors). Then, with the Brush tool, paint over the areas you want to show the colorize adjustment.**

   For the example, paint white everywhere except the lady's face and hand. As you can see in Figure 2-6, doing this saves on wardrobe and props.

Figure 2-6: When you want to highlight the foreground subject, try removing all the unique colors in the background.

 The little light bulb icons on palettes and in dialog boxes are for context-sensitive help pertaining to the command or palette controls in which you're working.

Making the Most of the Variations Feature

The Variations command enables you to selectively adjust colors and color-casting problems by clicking blue, red, and green variations of an image. It's invaluable for several reasons:

✦ You can see right in the command box the before and after versions of the photo.

✦ You can fine-tune color tolerances to make subtle to sweeping changes.

✦ You can control saturation and color casting in the shadows, midtones, and highlight ranges of the image.

Color opposites exist in computer graphics. However, unlike the color wheel in grade school, computer colors are *additive* — red, green, and blue combined at full intensity result in white. On the other hand, *subtractive* pigments (like crayons or house paint) combined result in black. Thus, the Variations command isn't exactly intuitive to use. Here's a little guide:

✦ **To reduce yellow:** Increase blue.

✦ **To reduce cyan:** Add its color opposite, red.

✦ **To reduce magenta:** Increase green.

> Outdoor film can add unwanted magenta to trees and grass; increasing green is the ticket.

Book III Chapter 2

Improving Color Balance

If you want to follow along with the example, open `DullBoatHouse.png`. Follow these steps to use the Variations feature to correct color casting in your image:

1. **Choose Enhance⇨Adjust Color⇨Color Variations.**

   The Color Variations dialog box opens.

2. **If the predominant areas of image detail are color casting to unwanted shades, you need to adjust the midtones. To do so, click the Midtones radio button and drag the Amount slider left to decrease the degree of variations or to the right to make more dramatic variations appear in the preview windows. Then click in the preview window to apply the change.**

   The midtones in the example image are fine.

3. **If the shady areas in your image are casting awful color shades, select the Shadows radio button and then click variation previews that look more visually pleasing.**

   In the example image, the shadow and highlight regions need some help. Leave the Amount slider at dead center. Click the Increase Green thumbnail once, and then again if you like "pound-you-over-the-head-green" in the image. The boat house turns a sickly color, so click Increase Red. Then click the Darken thumbnail to add some contrast to the image.

4. **If an image looks dull, you need to adjust the Highlights in the image. Select the Highlights radio button and then click the Lighten preview window. (You might have to click more than once to get the desired effect depending on the Amount slider's position.)**

    For the example, click the Increase Green thumbnail twice and then click Increase Red. Click the Lighten thumbnail once.

5. **If the image looks too vibrant or washed out, you need to adjust the Saturation. Select the Saturation radio button and then click the More or Less preview windows, depending on the problem.**

    The example image still needs more color. Select the Saturation radio button and then click the More Saturation thumbnail. See Figure 2-7 for a vastly improved image.

6. **When you're satisfied with your image, click OK to close the Color Varations dialog box.**

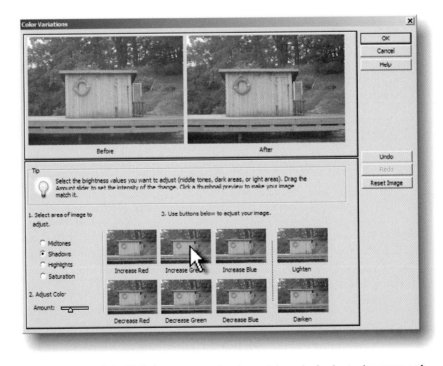

Figure 2-7: The Color Variations command makes quick work of color-tuning ranges of tones in an image.

Putting It Together

Creating Composition Focus with Color

In the steps to follow, you add some life to the colors in the `Load Balloons.png` image and then selectively colorize the image:

1. **Click the Quick Fix button and drag the Saturation slider a little to the right — say, one-eighth of an inch. Then drag the midtone contrast slider to the right by the same amount.**

Adjusting saturation and tones is often a hand-in-hand task. As you can see in the following figure, the image needed a little saturation and contrast.

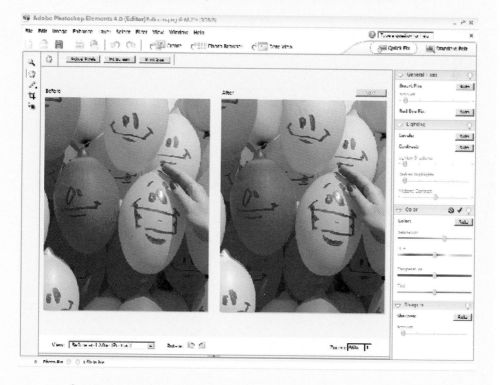

Book III
Chapter 2

Improving
Color Balance

2. **Click Editor mode at the top right of the screen.**

3. **Click the Adjustment Layer icon on the Layers palette and then choose Hue/Saturation.**

continued

continued

4. **In the Hue/Saturation command, click the Colorize check box and drag the Hue slider to 233, the Saturation slider to 36, and the Lightness slider to –6. Then click OK.**

In the following figure, the Colorize feature makes all the balloons the same hue. And the girl's hand; oops!

5. **With black as the foreground color on the Toolbox, choose the Paint tool; choose a 27 pixel tip from the Options bar.**

6. **Stroke over the girl's hand as well as the balloon she's caressing.**

7. **When you're done, right-click either Adjustment layer icon on the Layers palette and then choose Flatten Image from the contextual menu.**

The hand and the lucky balloon are the stars of the photo, as shown in the following figure.

Adjusting the colors in only part of an image directs the viewer's attention to where you want it.

Book IV
Creating and Using Selections

The 5th Wave   By Rich Tennant

"I'm going to assume that most of you – but not all of you – understand that this session on 'masking' has to do with Photoshop Elements."

Many average photos need only part of the picture modified. But to modify just a part of an image, you have to get hold of it. In Book IV, you gain experience with the Elements selection tools that allow you to isolate and then modify image areas. After you select something, you can drag it, paint on it, distort it, add to it, or remove from it. Say goodbye to the problems in your pictures and hello to the selection tools.

Chapter 1: Creating Basic Selections

In This Chapter

⮕ **Creating rectangular and elliptical selections**

⮕ **Adding to and subtracting from selections**

⮕ **Feathering selections**

⮕ **Copying selected image areas**

*P*hotos that you take fall into one of three categories: perfect ones (Elements is not required), awful ones (a wastebasket is required), and pictures that stand a little correcting in specific areas (for which Elements is the right medicine). Although Elements has the tools for both selecting and correcting image areas, before you run with the proverbial scissors, you need to master how to use the Elements "scissors" — the selection tools. This chapter takes you through basic selection tools: the Rectangular and Elliptical (an *oval* to non-Adobe employees) Marquee tools, with which you can crop photos and adjust or copy areas inside the selection marquees you find out how to create in this chapter.

Because few objects in life are perfectly rectangular or oval, Elements has special addition and subtraction modes with which you can modify an existing rectangular selection to make intricate polygons or make crescents from ovals. You can soften a selection edge to create a cameo-style picture by using feathering, and selections and layers go hand-in-hand; you can duplicate the contents of a selection to a layer, and from there create a very elaborate piece of work.

You can find all the files I use in this chapter at www.dummies.com/go/PhotoshopElementsAIOFD1e.

Understanding Selections

A *selection* defines an area within a photograph that you can modify with the Elements painting tools, tone and color commands, and filters. I need to park my scissors metaphor for a moment because an Elements selection is form without substance (sort of like a paperback from an airport gift shop). A selection is only the marker until you do something to the image beneath the selection. This book demystifies selections and puts their power where it belongs: at your cursor tip.

In Figure 1-1, the Rectangular and Elliptical Marquee tools are shown on the Toolbox. You drag on the face of the icon to reveal the type of selection tool you need. Or more simply, choose one of the tools and then you can choose the others from the Options bar.

You can reposition a marquee simply by dragging (with a selection tool) inside the selection. This doesn't affect the underlying image pixels at all.

Options bar

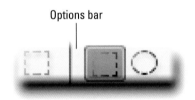

Toolbox

Figure 1-1: The Elements Marquee tools.

Using Marquee Selection Tools

A *marquee* is a visible screen element that tells you where you created a selection, so named because a selection appears in an image window with an animated dashed outline like a movie marquee. Marquee selection is performed by dragging the cursor diagonally. The interior of a marquee selection is available for editing, but image areas outside the selection are protected from editing, which is extremely handy when you want to edit only a section of a photo. The following sections go through how to create the selection types covered in this chapter.

Before you select a single rectangular or rounded shape, click the New Selection icon on the Options toolbar. Do this to ensure that Elements makes only one new selection instead of attempting to combine this shape with your previous selection. If you want to combine selections into a complex shape, I show you how later, in the upcoming section, "Adding to a selection."

Making square and rectangle selections

You have several options when you make a square and rectangle selection, including aspect ratio, fixed size, and feathering. Naturally, a rectangle selection is best used to describe the geometry of a rectangular object in a photo, such as a sheet of paper, a building, or a cardboard box; the following sections take you through choosing the appropriate basic selection tool to get quick and accurate results.

If the onscreen image is too small to accurately select the area you want, zoom in on the image to better show the area you want to select. See Book I, Chapter 1 to find out how to zoom.

If you're game to try out the Rectangular Marquee tool, you can use my ChessBored.png file; it has several squares in it.

1. **Choose the Rectangular Marquee tool and then place the cursor in a corner of what you want to capture as a rectangle.**

   In the ChessBored.png file, place your cursor at the upper-right corner of the chessboard image.

2. **Hold down the mouse button while you drag the cursor to the lower-left corner of the object you're selecting (the green square in this example).**

   Direction doesn't count; you could also drag from the top left to the bottom right of the object. The only important thing is that you drag diagonally, often called *marquee selecting*.

3. **Release the mouse button.**

   The selected area is marked onscreen by a marquee. In Figure 1-2, the onscreen marquee shows that the knight's square is selected, ready for filling, moving, filtering . . . you name it.

Doing something with the image area encompassed by the marquee is the next logical step. I cover that after going over the other selection options.

**Book IV
Chapter 1**

**Creating Basic
Selections**

Figure 1-2: Use the Rectangular Marquee tool to target rectangular or square areas in an image.

Adding to a selection

Suppose you want to select more than one rectangle in an image. A photo of a cardboard box with one flap open, and two different rectangular areas that don't meet are both candidates for using Add mode. Follow these steps to select multiple areas:

1. **Select the first rectangular area you want.**

2. **Click the Add to Selection icon on the Options bar, the second from left in the row of buttons.**

3. **Marquee-select the second rectangle.**

   You now have two visible marquees in the image, as shown in Figure 1-3, but it's really one selection — if you move the marquee by dragging inside the image with any selection tool, the two marquees move as one.

Figure 1-3: The two marquees represent a single selection.

In Add to Selection mode, you can continue to add to your existing selection, eventually selecting a whole image although pressing Ctrl+A would be simpler if that's your intention.

When you select an area that overlaps another selected area, Elements automatically puts the marquee around the combined area of both selections, instead of showing the separate selected areas.

Using a grid to help select objects

The Elements Grid feature can help you enormously with selection precision. Using a Grid can guide your selection tool to a defined beginning and end point as you drag. If the default Grid frequency doesn't suit your particular needs, you can customize it. To use the grid, you have to choose View➪Grid to make it visible. Using a grid usually goes hand in hand with enabling the View➪Snap to Grid command; your selection will then be guided to the closest grid mark when you begin and end a selection. If the Snap option is turned off, by all means turn it on when you need a grid-accurate selection.

In the following steps, I show you how to set up and use a grid; you'll see how accurately and quickly you can define a rectangular selection. You can use the `ChessBored.png` file from earlier in this chapter.

1. **Click the Normal (the default) selection mode icon, the far-left button in the group on the Options bar.**

   You'll mess up your work if you don't reset the selection mode. It's easy to forget which mode your selection tool is in.

2. **Press Ctrl+D to deselect the current selection.**

3. **Press Ctrl+K to take you to Elements Preferences.**

4. **Choose Grid from the Preferences dialog box to see the options shown in Figure 1-4.**

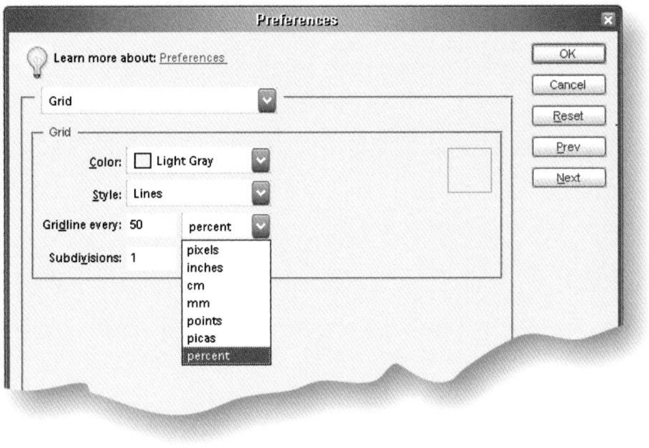

Figure 1-4: Adjust the grid options to make the grid appear exactly the way you want it to.

You set your preferences for grid display here. Color can be an important option — you wouldn't want to define a blue grid when working on an image that's mostly blue, for example. Dashed lines are less visually intrusive than the default lines option, and dots are still less intrusive. But the important option in this box is the frequency of the grid — how many gridlines and how many subdivisions you specify has an impact on selection accuracy.

For this example, set the grid to 25% (you can choose pixels or other increments, but I find percentage to be intuitive and quick to work with) and 1 subdivision, and then close the dialog box. These settings will come in handy when used with a variety of images.

5. Choose View⇨Grid and then View⇨Snap to Grid.

Now when you put your cursor on the grid intersection of any of the squares in the image, hold Alt, and then drag to the edge of the image window. You draw the marquee selection from the center outward (because you used the Alt modifier key), as shown in Figure 1-5. Many times, it's easier to drag a selection from the center outward, especially when your view in an image window is obscured because it's too small, you've got a palette floating over part of the image window, or when you want a selection centered.

Figure 1-5: Use the Alt key to select from the center out.

You have to use the Alt key for dragging selections from the center because Elements doesn't have a funny little icon for a draw-from-center option.

If a selection is already in the image, holding Alt subtracts from the existing selection.

Setting a fixed aspect ratio

If you want to drag rectangles that are squares (and ovals that are perfect circles), use the Fixed Aspect Ratio option on the Options bar. Here's how to make a square marquee selection. You can use the ChessBored.png file from earlier in this chapter.

1. Choose Fixed Aspect Ratio from the Mode drop-down box on the Options bar.

By default, 1-to-1 proportions are chosen, which are perfect for the purpose of selecting a square on the chessboard of the ChessBored. png file.

Aspect ratios can help you out a lot when cropping an image to size for a physical picture frame; you're not limited to the default 1:1 option. For example, if you have a 5" x 7" picture frame, set the aspect ratio to Width:5 and Height:7, crop away (on a copy of your photo) and then print it. Similarly, 4" x 6" and 8" x 10" photos can be created for your picture frames. If you have a tall picture instead of a wide one, simply click the swap icon between the fields on the Options bar after you've entered the dimensions you want. See the following section for more info.

2. **Drag from top left to bottom right over any square (chess square, in this example).**

   You get a 1:1 square selection.

   In Figure 1-6, you can see the result of using Fixed Aspect Ratio.

Figure 1-6: Elements lets you make perfectly square selections.

Cropping to an aspect ratio

You can also crop a selection to only part of an image by creating a selection to the proportions you want and then choosing Edit➪Crop. For example, suppose you want to crop part of an image and print it to 5" x 7". To crop an image to specific proportions, follow these steps:

1. **Choose Fixed Aspect Ratio from the Options bar Mode drop-down menu, and type the width you want in the Width field and the height in the Height field.**

   For this example, you can enter **5** for width and **7** for height, respectively, for a portrait-oriented 5" x 7" image.

2. **Drag in the image window.**

   As you can see in Figure 1-7, the Marquee tool constrains to the dimensions you want.

   If you want a wide picture (landscape-oriented) and not a tall one (portrait), click the swap height and width icon between the two fields on the Options bar; then drag your marquee.

3. **Choose Image➪Crop.**

4. **Save the file.**

   For printing a photo, save it in PNG or TIFF format. Save the modified file under a new name unless you want to replace the original file.

Figure 1-7: Crop to an aspect ratio for a set size.

Using the Fixed Size selection option

You use the Fixed Size mode option for pictures you want to post on the Web, for example, in forums that limit image dimensions. You might not use the Fixed Size mode option often (because Web images usually need to be scaled as well as cropped), but it's great if you need a section of a very large image — to use as desktop wallpaper, for example. Here's how to make such a grand selection:

1. **Choose Fixed Size from the Mode drop-down list on the Options bar. Type the dimensions of your monitor resolution in the Width and Height fields.**

   1024 px (pixels) by 768 px is a common dimension pairing.

   Elements defaults to pixels (px) for Fixed Size mode. Unless you want to select in inches (in which case, you enter **in** after a space after your number), you don't need to type a unit of measurement after the numbers you enter.

2. **Click the upper-left corner where you want the selection — but don't drag.**

3. **Choose Image⇨Crop.**

4. **For desktop wallpaper, save the image to BMP, JPEG, PNG, or GIF (not recommended because it's limited to 256 colors) format, the only formats Windows XP and Vista accept.**

5. **Save your cropped file to** `C:\Windows`.

6. **Load your wallpaper the standard Windows way.**

Creating circle and oval selections

Use the Elliptical Marquee tool to select round areas, such as circles and ovals. This tool works like the Rectangle Marquee tool except that these selections have curved edges and no corners. In a nutshell, you just marquee-drag using the tool. If you skipped the earlier section on selecting rectangles, hop back there to see how easy this is. You constrain selection proportions just as you do with the Rectangular Marquee tool, and also add and subtract areas by using the Options bar controls.

You can also drag ovals that are perfect circles by using the Fixed Aspect Ratio option on the Options bar, 1:1 ratio, although holding Shift while you drag accomplishes the same thing. To create cameo-style crops for, say, an 8" x 10" frame, you'd enter **8** and **10** in the width and height fields, respectively, drag the ellipse, press Ctrl+Shift+I to invert the selection, and fill it with the desired color (***Hint:*** White is best because it doesn't print and saves ink.) Then press Ctrl+Shift+I and choose Edit⇨Crop. Elements crops to the outer edges of the selection.

For practice doing something with a selection, you can follow along with my `Marbles.png` file, which features several circular objects, ideal for selecting with the Elliptical Marquee tool. Read on to see how to create a circular selection and copy the underlying image area.

1. **Choose the Elliptical tool.**

   You don't have to necessarily visit the Elements Toolbox to fetch the Elliptical tool, if you just used the Rectangular tool. Just click the Elliptical Marquee tool on the Options bar.

   You can also go ahead and choose your Fixed Aspect Ratio now. For this example, choose 1:1. See the earlier section, "Setting a fixed aspect ratio," for more on this.

2. **Marquee-select an object in the image (one of the marbles, if you're using my file).**

   For help on making a selection, see the earlier section, "Using Marquee Selection Tools."

3. **(Optional) If necessary, reposition the marquee.**

   Reposition a marquee simply by dragging (using a selection tool) inside the selection.

4. **To create a duplicate of the object**

   a. *Switch to the Move tool (Ctrl+V).*

   b. *Hold Shift+Alt and drag the marquee.*

   You create a duplicate of the marble. The duplicate is floating on the image; it's not part of the background.

5. To make the new marble a permanent part of the image background, as shown in Figure 1-8, press Ctrl+D.

Figure 1-8: Watch your marble collection grow!

6. To move the duplicate marble to a layer of its own

a. Make your selection. This trick works with any selection tool.

b. Right-click in the selection.

c. Choose Layer via Copy from the contextual menu.

Bang, the marble gets a layer just to itself, the Background layer is unperturbed, and you can now reposition the duplicate marble for weeks on end, like I did in Figure 1-9.

Figure 1-9: A selection isn't much good unless you put it to use!

Making Selection Transformations

Elliptical and rectangular marquee selections are created parallel to the image window, which isn't very helpful if you need to illustrate a beryllium atom, whose orbiting electrons need to travel at an angle!

To make a diagonal elliptical selection, you need to first make an ellipse, fill it, and then use Free Transform on the filled selection. Then you load the selection based on the transformed, filled object, choose the layer to which you want to copy, fill, or stroke, and create your magic. Try these moves out in a new, blank image window (choose Transparent in the Background Contents drop-down list in the New dialog box):

1. **Drag a tallish ellipse selection and then press Alt+Backspace to fill it with foreground color (any color will do).**

2. **Press Ctrl+T (Free Transform).**

3. **Hover your cursor over a corner of the Free Transform bounding box until your cursor becomes a bent arrow shape.**

4. **Drag up or down on the bounding box corner, as shown in Figure 1-10.**

   For precision rotating, type a value in the Rotate field on the Options bar.

5. **Press Enter to apply the rotation.**

   You could be done now, but say you don't want a filled selection but a different fill color or a stroked outline instead.

6. **On the Layers palette, make the Opacity 0%, so you can see what you're doing in the steps to follow.**

   Selections and layers go hand in hand. For the lowdown on layers, see Book V, Chapter 1.

Figure 1-10: Tilt your ellipse by dragging a corner handle.

7. **Ctrl-click the layer thumbnail to load the layer's pixels as a selection; then click the New Layer icon (the dog-eared page icon at the top left).**

   You're working on a brand-new layer — no strokes, no fills, but only the active, rotated ellipse selection.

   The rotated marquee selection can now be filled or stroked from the Edit menu. To do so

   a. *Press D (Default colors; black is your current foreground color now).*

b. *Choose Edit⇨Stroke (Outline) Selection.*

c. *Type a value in the Width field. If your image is small, 3 (pixels in width) will be visible. For 4MB images or larger, increase the width; 6 or 7 works well for a thin but visible outline stroke.*

d. *Click OK.*

You created an electron orbit, as shown in Figure 1-11. I know you're excited, but beryllium has four electrons, four protons, and four neutrons (I'm not a prophead; I just Googled *beryllium*), so use the techniques already discussed to complete the atom, if you like.

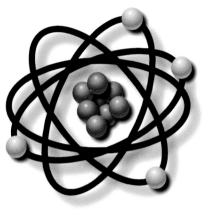

Figure 1-11: Add a few more ellipses and some simple spheres, and you've got yourself some beryllium.

Combining Selection Techniques

If you've followed the chapter to this point, you have the skill to create a *composite* selection — one that starts with a base selection that you add to, subtract from, and so on to make a complex shape. Combining different selection shapes is your key to building elegant shapes, such as the wrench in the following example. By using the Add To and Subtract From modes with a combination of elliptical and rectangular selections, you can create just about any selection to then fill or stroke. Follow these steps to run through a method for creating a wrench-shaped selection.

1. **Ctrl+double-click on the work-space to create a new image window — any size will do.**

2. **Drag a circle (an ellipse with Fixed Aspect Ratio turned on).**

   Read about Fixed Aspect Ratio ear-lier in this chapter.

3. **Drag a second circle about one circle length below the first with Add To mode turned on.**

   You end up with two circular marquees representing a single selection, as shown in Figure 1-12.

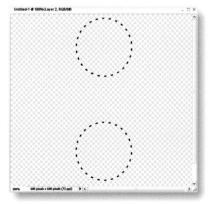

Figure 1-12: These two circles are a single selection.

4. **Choose the Rectangle Marquee tool, also in Add To mode, and connect the two circle selections by dragging just inside the bottom of the top circle to just inside the top of the bottom circle.**

   Work with me here; think *wrench* — you're creating the handle.

5. **Use Subtract mode in combination with the rectangle tool to put the notches in the top and bottom heads of your new wrench selection.**

6. **(Optional) For fun, choose the Gradient tool, right-click in the selection to display the Gradient palette, and choose Metals from the flyout collection list.**

7. **Choose any gradient you like and then drag at an angle in the image window. See Figure 1-13.**

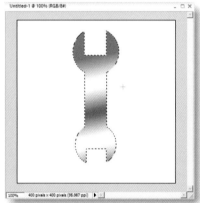

 Selections not only precisely pick out image areas, but they also confine fills to just the selection — no spills, no need to keep hand wipes next to your workstation.

Figure 1-13: Combine selection shapes to build complex shapes.

Feathering Selections

Feathering is the softening of the edge of a selection. In other words, a clearly defined selection edge takes on a transition between fully selected and not selected — you specify the amount (distance) of feathering in pixels or inches.

You can add feathering by either

✦ **Right-clicking in a selection when a selection tool is chosen.**

   or

✦ **Typing a Feather value on the Options bar before you create a selection,** which often leads to trouble.

   I don't recommend doing this because if you forget to delete the Feather value, every selection you create in the future with the selection tool feathers the selection. The marquee of a feathered selection looks identical to an unfeathered one; usually in image editing, you don't want feathering.

Here's how to feather a selection around a portrait to create a soft-edge cameo picture:

1. **Drag a marquee around your subject. Reposition the selection if it's not dead-center.**

   I opted for an elliptical selection, like a vignette photo.

2. **Right-click and choose Feather from the contextual menu.**

   The Feather Selection dialog box pops up, where you enter the Feather Radius, as shown in Figure 1-14.

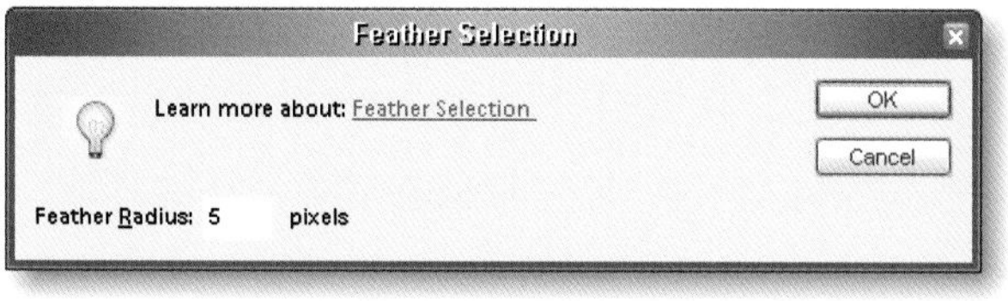

![Feather Selection dialog box showing a light bulb icon, "Learn more about: Feather Selection", OK and Cancel buttons, and "Feather Radius: 5 pixels".]

Figure 1-14: Enter a feather radius in the Feather Selection dialog box.

3. **Enter the feather radius.**

   How much feathering you need depends on the image size and how spectacular you want the effect to be. For 1MB images, no more than 15 pixels will do.

4. **Click OK to apply the feathering.**

   You probably won't notice a change in the marquee, but the selection has been feathered.

5. **To see the effect of feathering, the underlying image needs to have the feathering applied to it. Right-click and choose Layer via Copy from the contextual menu.**

6. **On the Layers palette, click the Background layer to make it the current editing layer.**

7. **Fill the entire background with your current foreground color on the Toolbox by pressing Ctrl+A and then Alt+Backspace.**

   See the results in Figure 1-15. (This tech editor's picture looks great for printing or putting up on the wall at my local post office.) Instead of a foreground color, I used the Styles and Effects palette texture collection; learn more about textures in Book V, Chapter 1.

Figure 1-15: Feathering adds a touch of class to any portrait.

Intersecting Selections

Intersecting selections produce a new shape where two or more shapes overlap. Intersecting selections are difficult or impossible to create with a single selection tool: namely, the elliptical, rectangular, or the freeform selection tools (covered in Chapter 2 of this mini-book).

You can make palm leaves, coffee beans, a cat's eye . . . the sky's the limit after you practice this technique.

As an example, the following steps show how to create a cat's-eye selection:

1. **Drag a circular selection in the left of an image window.**

 2. **Click the Intersection mode icon on the Options bar, the far-right button in the group.**

3. **From right to left (again, you can marquee-select in any direction), drag a second selection that intersects the existing selection.**

   In Figure 1-16, the result is a cat's-eye shape. Intersecting two ellipses leaves you with an ellipse with points at both ends.

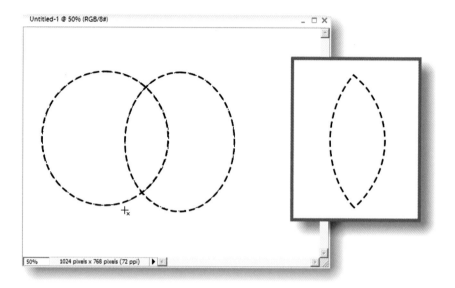

Figure 1-16: Intersecting selections produce a new shape where two or more shapes overlap.

Tapping into the Select Menu

The Select⇨Modify⇨Expand, Contract, and Border commands can modify any type of selection. Here's a brief explanation of each and when you might want to use each:

+ **Select⇨Modify⇨Expand:** Expands the perimeter of the current selection. Use it for increasing the size of the current selection.

+ **Select⇨Modify⇨Contract:** Contracts the perimeter of the current selection. Use it for decreasing the size of the current selection. This is very useful for eliminating fringing (see Book V, Chapter 1).

+ **Select⇨Modify⇨Border:** This command can turn an ellipse selection into a ring selection, for example. Unfortunately, Elements feathers the modified border selection, and there's no easy way around it. (Read about feathering earlier in this chapter.)

Here's an example of how to use Border to put a soft-edged halo above a subject in an image:

1. **Drag an ellipse in the image.**

2. **Choose Select⇨Modify⇨Border.**

3. **In the dialog box, choose a border width of about 25 pixels and then click OK.**

The exact value for your image depends on the intensity of the effect you want and the image size.

4. **Fill the selection with a light foreground color; choose the color from the Color Picker.**

   I chose a gold color for the halo.

5. **Press Alt+Backspace to fill the selection with foreground color, as shown in Figure 1-17.**

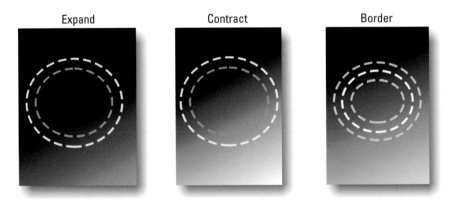

| Expand | Contract | Border |

Figure 1-17: The halo begins to take shape.

6. **Put a still lighter color in the middle of the halo by first choosing Select⇨Modify⇨ Contract.**

7. **Choose 12 pixels (about half the width of your 25-pixel Border modification in Step 3) for the contraction and then click OK.**

8. **Fill the contracted selection with near-white or any shade that's lighter than the existing color in the image.**

   Figure 1-18 shows the results.

Figure 1-18: This halo can make anyone an angel.

Here is a second way to create a halo, but unlike the Border command, this method produces a hard-edged ring:

1. **Create an oval selection and then choose Select⇨Save Selection.**

2. **Name the selection something evocative, such as *Ring*.**

   A selection disappears when you click outside it in standard Select mode. You can't easily retrieve a selection if you haven't saved it.

3. **Choose Select⇨Modify⇨Contract and accept the value you used last: 12 pixels. Click OK.**

Saving selections to alpha channels

Selection information can be written to an image channel in addition to the component RGB color channels of a photo. (An alpha channel isn't an off-color cable TV channel.) You can't peer into an image channel by using Elements, but the selection information is indeed there when you save a selection. Other programs can read saved selections:

- Photoshop CS2 and other paint programs (such as Corel Painter) can read and modify a saved selection (alpha) channel that was written by Elements.

- Elements can load a selection saved from an alpha channel using other applications.

Today, alpha channels aren't used as much as image layers because you can see the visual contents of a layer and load opaque areas as a marquee selection. But you'll find times when you'll prefer to save a selection to an alpha channel.

Elements can save 56 alpha channels when you save an image to the native PSD file format and up to 32 in TIFF format, but other applications might only be able to read but a single one. And other applications might display alpha information as image transparency information, so be careful when you save selections if you're going to use other apps for editing and viewing an image.

4. **Choose Select⇨Save Selection and then choose Ring from the Selection drop-down list.**

5. **In the Operation field, choose Subtract from Selection and then click OK.**

6. **Choose Select⇨Load Selection, choose Ring from the drop-down Selection box, and then click OK.**

In Figure 1-19, on the right, I dragged the Gradient tool in Circular Fill mode (on the Options bar) from the center of the selection outward. See how different the result is from the filled Border command at left.

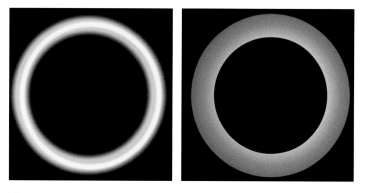

Figure 1-19: There's more than one way to get your halo. Donating to the Salvation Army is another one.

Using Selection Techniques Together

The following example uses all the techniques from this chapter to create a machine gear:

1. **In a new image window, make a circle selection.**

2. **Save and then contract the selection.**

3. **Save the selection under the same name, subtracting from the saved selection, and then load the saved selection.**

   The following figure shows the results.

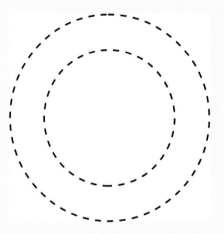

4. **With the Rectangle Marquee in Add To mode, drag a rectangle to intersect with the top center of the selection. Do the same at 3, 6, and 9 o'clock. Save the new selection under the same name.**

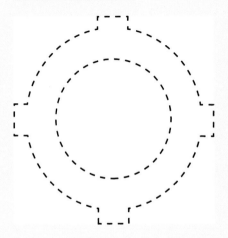

5. With the selection still active, press Alt+Backspace to fill it. Press Ctrl+T for the Free Transform feature and type 45 in the Rotate field of the Options bar.

This rotates the image 45 degrees.

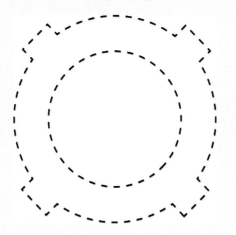

6. Repeat Step 4 to add four more notches to the gear. Save the new gear selection.

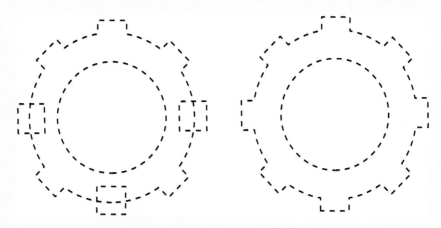

7. Fill the selection with a metallic gradient.

continued

Book IV
Chapter 1

Creating Basic
Selections

continued

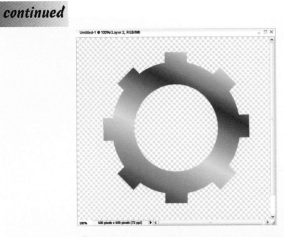

8. With a Marquee tool chosen, right-click and select Copy via Layer.

9. Add a bevel effect to the gear (use the Styles and Effects palette) and perhaps a nice drop shadow effect to lift the gear off the page.

Chapter 2: Creating Freeform Selections

In This Chapter

- ✔ Lassoing selections
- ✔ Creating polygon selections
- ✔ Erasing by color similarity
- ✔ Brushing on a selection
- ✔ Tapping into anti-aliasing
- ✔ Creating a layered composition

Most images have plenty of swoops, curves, and irregular edges, and Elements has the editing prowess to select these irregular shapes. You'll have this prowess, too, after you master which tool does what. Elements offers several categories of tools for making freeform selections, including lassos, erasers, brushes, and more.

The ability to make a selection gives you extra flexibility in editing your images. After making a selection, you can

- ✦ Restrict painting, cloning, and other editing to one or more areas. (Book I, Chapter 3 covers painting in more detail, and Book VI, Chapter 2 covers cloning.)

- ✦ Copy areas to a layer. (See Book V, Chapter 1 for details on working with layers.)

- ✦ Delete everything outside the selection.

In the sections that follow, you gain hands-on experience in selecting areas of an image with all these freeform selection tools. I also explain options and tools that result in more natural-looking selections, such as anti-aliasing and removing a fringe (an unwanted halo) around a selection after you copy it to a new background.

You can find all the files I use in this chapter at www.dummies.com/go/
PhotoshopElementsAIOFD1e.

Corralling Selections with the Lasso Tools

One important set of tools for making freeform selections in Elements is the lasso tools, as shown in Figure 2-1. You find them on the Tools palette, with the Lasso tool on top and the Polygonal Lasso tool underneath. (You also find the Magnetic Lasso, which I cover in Book IV, Chapter 3, along with the other tools that make selections based on a color range.) In the sections that follow, I explain how to use these tools to select different types of objects.

Figure 2-1: Freeform selection tools can help you choose only a part of an image to change.

Selecting with the Lasso tool

In the upcoming Figure 2-2, I made a selection with the Lasso tool. Everything inside the dashed line is selected and ready for whatever you'd like to do to this area. And everything outside this visual onscreen indicator is protected against changes.

The most frequent use of the Lasso tool is to create freeform, initial selections that you refine later using the other selection tools within Elements.

To use the Lasso tool, here are the steps to follow:

1. **Select the Lasso tool, either by clicking it in the Tools palette or pressing Shift+L (which toggles through the Lasso tool group) until the Lasso tool is selected.**

2. **Drag around an image area you want selected, as shown in Figure 2-2.**

   You can select the cracker crumbs shown in Figure 2-2 to remove them, for example.

3. **Close the selection by releasing the mouse button at your beginning point.**

Selected area

Figure 2-2: The Lasso tool is great for selecting irregular image shapes.

If for some reason you prematurely release the mouse button, a Lasso selection auto-closes, creating a straight line where you left off, connecting to your beginning point. This is often unwanted; to manually correct the shape of the selection, hold the Shift key and add to the selection by dragging around the area you intended to select.

Cornering the Polygonal Lasso tool

The Polygonal Lasso tool creates straight-edged selections. You click points in an image to shape the selection and then close the selection at the beginning point to close (and activate) it.

You'll use this tool most often to select areas in an image that feature architecture because buildings typically have straight edges. It's also a good tool to use when selecting boxes — and other polygons.

Here's something you should know before choosing the Polygonal Lasso tool: It's sticky. After you complete a polygonal selection, it wants to start a new selection anywhere you click. To disable this sticky behavior (and to further your Elements prowess), try choosing the plain Lasso tool and then holding Alt while you click around an image. Doing this toggles to the Polygonal Lasso tool; when you release the mouse button after making a polygon selection and release Alt, no further selections are begun. However, you cannot add, subtract, or create an intersection with an existing selection using the Lasso while you're holding Alt. When you want to modify a polygon selection with another polygon selection, you have to choose the Polygonal Lasso — not the Lasso+Alt trick.

To make a selection with the Polygonal Lasso, follow these steps:

1. **Open the image where you want to make a selection and zoom in until you can clearly see the edge of the geometry you want to select.**

   To see the overall image and have a close-up view within which to work, choose View⇨New Window. A second window appears, where you can see the whole image.

2. **Select the Polygonal Lasso tool in the Tools palette.**

   Do so by dragging on the face of the tool to reveal the whole group and then choose the tool from the group.

3. **Click a corner along the edge of the area you want to select.**

4. Continue clicking points at the corners, such as the building corners shown in Figure 2-3.

Hold the spacebar and drag to pan the window, if needed, to click corners and remain zoomed in.

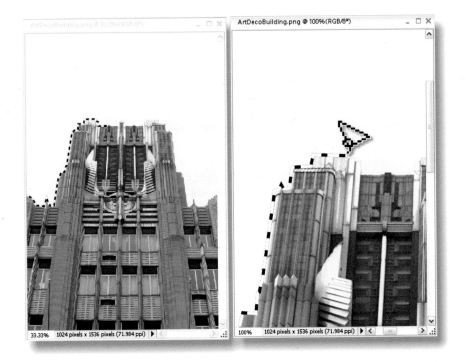

Figure 2-3: The Polygonal Lasso tool is ideal for selecting architecture.

5. When you complete selecting from your current view, click at the point where you started the selection, or double-click to close the beginning point.

Naturally, you'll want to do something with a selection you create, so the following steps show you how to replace the blah sky in the building image with a better sky:

1. Double-click the thumbnail on the Layers palette (accept the default name in the New Layer dialog box and click OK).

You can close the duplicate image window, if you have one open.

As I mention earlier, the contents of a selection are subject to change (painting, copying, deleting) while the areas at the exterior of a selection